Revenue Raiders: Macon County's Whiskey War

By

CL Gammon

DRP

Deep Read Press

LAFAYETTE, TENNESSEE

www.deepreadpress.com

ISBN: 978-1-954989-13-9

Edited by: Shena Newberry Wilder

Cover Design by: Kim Gammon

Published by:

DEEP READ PRESS

Lafayette, Tennessee

www.deepreadpress.com

For Shelta McCarter Shrum

Acknowledgements

I have received a great deal of help, directly and indirectly, in the preparation of this book. As always, the staff of Deep Read Press has worked diligently to make it better. They have succeeded.

This book would not have been possible without the help Shelta McCarter Shrum gave me. Beyond the mass of materials Shelta provided, she answered my questions patiently and with good humor.

June Shrum of the Macon County Historical Society took time out from her duties and answered a great many questions I posed to her in my many telephone calls. She went out of her way to help me and I am grateful to her.

Barry Witcher provided some insights into one of the articles in this book.

Michael Meador agreed to allow me to use the photo of Joe Cartwright.

I would also like to thank the good folk at the Tennessee Electronic Library for providing thousands of items to researchers, including me, free of charge.

I am sure there are others that I am forgetting to thank for their help. To them, I apologize.

The above being said, I alone am responsible for any errors that may be contained within the pages of this book.

CL Gammon

Table of Contents

Introduction

"Whiskey probably goes to the head because that is where those who drink much of it have the most room for it." – **Macon County News, 1913**.

Alcohol use and abuse is a problem as old as humankind is. Trying to cope with it is no more than one day younger. Combating the problem with legislation has had mixed results at best, and fighting it through education hasn't succeeded all that well either.

Tennessee enacted the nation's first prohibition statute on January 26, 1838, and enacted several liquor laws throughout the decades. They also employed hundreds of raiders to ferret out and shut down illegal distilleries. Yet, stills continued to pop up like crabgrass on an otherwise beautiful lawn.

Over the decades, moonshiners, bootleggers, and rumrunners have taken on the mantle of anti-heroes. They have been Romanized in old movies like *Thunder Road* and *Smoky and the Bandit*. NASCAR still claims a kinship with fast driving moonshiners of old. A soft drink bears the name "Mountain Dew." Songs and even institutions of higher education glorify them. For instance, the fight song of the University of

Tennessee refers to moonshiners and (by implication) to the murder of revenuers.

The truth is that far from being a romantic endeavor, running 'shine was dangerous business. Interdicting the flow of illicit alcohol was dangerous too, as the body count in the whisky war proves sadly.

This book deals with the efforts to curb the illicit liquor trade in one small Tennessee county – that of Macon – between 1877 and 1941. The 69 short articles illustrating those efforts represent but a tiny fraction of the events that took place during the whiskey war. Make no mistake about it – it was a real war. As with all wars, it had real casualties and a real death toll. All sides suffered immensely from it.

By the way, the author chooses to report on the war in an unbiased manner. Taking sides helps no one.

This book lists names of those involved. However, old newspapers, especially from Nashville were sometimes haphazard with the spellings of names. The author does not pretend to be able to magically discern if a given spelling is correct or not and unless he knew a given name was listed with an incorrect spelling, he left it as it was presented in the original newspaper article or book.

In the preparation of this book, the author has waded through thousands of newspaper articles and scores of books, and has given only a very few of the highlights. A comprehensive account of everyone involved in the whiskey war over the almost seven decades this book covers, even if it were possible, would take up several volumes.

The author sincerely hopes the reader will be able to take something positive away from this book.

I. 1870-1879

The Revenue Raiders were very active in the 1870s in the dangerous wilds of Macon County. They captured a good many wildcat distilleries and moonshiners. They also faced death from moonshiners who would gladly kill to preserve their illegal businesses.

Included in this section are ten articles from the 1870s that illustrate the war on liquor in Macon County at that time. They also illustrate the fact that raiders sometimes went too far in the pursuit of their duty.

A look at the locations of the distilleries found in 1870s Macon County proves how widespread whiskey making was. Practically any secluded place with a large stream of fresh water nearby was likely to be the site of a wildcat whiskey operation.

1. Massive Liquor Raids

The war against independent moonshiners began long before National Prohibition. While Federal Marshalls in the American West chased after bandits and cattle rustlers, in Tennessee they spent much of their time breaking up wildcat distilleries and collecting revenues.

Today, when we think of moonshine operations, we think of "rotgut" whiskey.

Revenue agents referred to independent liquor operators as "wildcats" or "wildcatters." Wildcat operations made and sold hundreds of thousands gallons of illegal drink in Tennessee each year.

Wildcats had moonshine stills running wide-open across middle Tennessee and in November 1877, the authorities put together a team of agents to raid wildcat distilleries in Sumner and Macon Counties. The hope was that the raids would slow the stream of illicit alcohol flooding the area,

The team consisted of United States Deputy Federal Marshalls James M. Davis, M. L. Kiggins, John L. Allen, John J. Bryan, Martin Davis, and two others. The raiders armed themselves with Spencer and Winchester rifles and left Nashville on November 21, 1877.

They struck in Sumner County first and had good success. The raiders did even better after crossing over into Macon County. In fact, their raids had phenomenal results.

The first distillery the raiders struck in Macon County was that of James Waldron. There they found 2 150-gallon stills and worms, 11 tubs, 900 gallons of beer, 20 bushels of cornmeal, 10 gallons of singlings, 10 gallons of whiskey, and 2 bushels of malt. The total value the raiders put on the operation was $500. The revenuers arrested Waldron and the judge bound him over for trial.

The raiders next descended upon the distillery operated by John Humphries. There they found a 150-gallon still, 1,100 gallons of beer, 10 gallons of whiskey, and 10 gallons of singlings. When Humphries saw the band of revenuers, he made for the hills. The posse chased after him and one member even took a shot at the escaping wildcatter, but Humphries escaped.

The gang of Federal agents next worked their way through the Long Creek community. Within the community, they located three distilleries. The moonshiners operating independently of each other were Hugh Alexander, Tandy Fishburn, and Dob Harwell. Between them, the distilleries had three 150-gallon copper stills, 5,700 gallons of beer and mash, 250 gallons of whiskey, 300 gallons of singlings, and a large amount of malt and cornmeal. The value of those three distilleries was about $1,500.

It was late when the Deputies finished with their raids for the day and they made camp for the night out in the open. A good many people living in the hills of Macon County had intense hostility toward the revenuers. Several people made noise throughout the night, and one even fired a weapon trying to intimidate the lawmen. The ploy irritated the officers, but it did not frighten the Deputies.

At some point during the evening, four men hostile to the raiders came into the camp. The raiders "arrested" the unwanted visitors and held them overnight. The next morning, they released the intruders.

At first light, the raiders broke camp and started back for Nashville, but along the way, they busted several other illicit liquor operations.

James Waldron eventually received a $100 fine and a sentence of 30 days in the Macon County Jail. Hugh Alexander too, received a jail sentence.

A problem arose over Macon County Sheriff James A. McDonald's "manner of carrying out the sentence of Waldron and Alexander." The problem led to a Federal officer arresting Sheriff McDonald on May 2, 1878 and charging him with contempt of court.

Sources.

Blankenship, Harold G. *History of Macon County, Tennessee*. Tompkinsville, Kentucky: Monroe County Press, 1986, page 155.

"Conflict of Jurisdiction." *Daily American*, January 3, 1879, page 1. Courtesy of the Tennessee Electronic Library.

"Raiding the Wild Cat." *Daily American*, November 27, 1877, page 4. Courtesy of the Tennessee Electronic Library.

"Sheriff Arrested For Contempt." *Daily American*, May 5, 1878, page 1. Courtesy of the Tennessee Electronic Library.

"The Courts." *Daily American*, April 25, 1878, page 4. Courtesy of the Tennessee Electronic Library.

2. More Raids on Long Creek

The revenue raiders continued their work in Macon County in early January 1878. The crewmembers for this set of raids were Deputies James M. Davis, John J. Bryan, J. J. Smith, Robert Brown, Charles Drain, and two others.

On January 9, the raiders struck in Macon County's Long Creek community again. The Deputies located and captured the distillery Hugh Alexander operated. They found a copper still and worm, 15 tubs, 1,500 gallons of beer and mash, 5 gallons of whiskey, and 100 gallons of singlings. The raiders had no good means to transport the items mentioned, so, they destroyed them.

The Deputies arrested Alexander and took him before the United States Commissioner at Hartsville and the Commissioner ordered the moonshiner jailed.

They made another raid along Long Creek, this time netting a distillery owned by Ben Parsons and a man named McCormack. The Deputies destroyed 24 tubs, 24,000 gallons of beer, 1 copper still with worm, 60 bushels of corn, and 100 gallons of singlings. The still owners also found themselves incarcerated.

The third raid took the still, 21 tubs, and 10 gallons of whiskey belonging to James Gibson. Gibson got away from the raiders with the worm. The raiders hacked the remainder of the still to pieces.

Source.

"Death On Wild-Cat." *Daily American*, January 12, 1878, page 4. Courtesy of the Tennessee Electronic Library.

3. Winter Raids

James M. Davis and his merry men continued their raids in the winter of 1878. On February 2, they moved into Macon County by way of Jackson County. As usual, they found stills and busted them up.

They found and chopped up John Denom's still. T. Whitley removed his still, but the raiders destroyed everything else at the distillery. They also found evidence of the removal of another distillery, but they could not identify the operator.

In Lafayette, the court bound over J. A. White and E. B. Meador for failure to pay the special alcohol tax.

The raiders were destroying stills and jailing moonshiners all over middle Tennessee, but the amount of illegal whiskey drenching the area continued to grow. Federal Commissioner Raum felt that more needed doing to put a cork in the alcohol flow in his district. Commissioner Raum informed Collector W. M. Woodcock that he had doubled the appropriation for the suppression of illicit whiskey in the district for the next 90 days.

Raum also approved Woodcock's forceful recommendation to grant James M. Davis a pay raise due to the Deputy's "faithful, fearless and efficient discharge of his duties." The bump in pay was substantial. The Deputy new annual salary was $2,400.

Sources.

"Moonshine Matters." *Daily American*, January 15, 1879, page 4. Courtesy of the Tennessee Electronic Library.

"The Wild-Cat War." *Daily American*, February 10, 1878, page 4. Courtesy of the Tennessee Electronic Library.

4. Raiders Indicted

Deputy Davis and his raiding revenue men were unpopular in many quarters. The dislike grew stronger when allegations that the raiders had abused their power and committed criminal offensives against the alleged moonshiners.

When James M. Davis and his men made their first raids in Macon County, even though they had no state or federal warrants, they detained and held several men overnight. They then released the detainees the next morning without filing any charges against them.

The arrested men felt abused and they went before a Grand Jury asking for indictments against some of the raiders.

Deputy Davis defended the actions of the raiders. He said that on the evening of the first raids in Macon County, while they camped, his men were afraid that the moonshiners would descend from the hills and attack them. Davis continued that the men he ordered detained came into the camp as a reconnoitering party. According to him, they intended to gain information about the raiders. This would make it easier for the moonshiners in the hills to launch a successful attack. The Deputy stated he felt it prudent to arrest the men, hold them overnight, and then release them the next morning.

In January 1878, the Grand Jury issued four indictments each against, Deputies Davis, M. L. Kiggins, and John J. Bryan. The Sheriff of Trousdale County served warrants on the trio and they each put up $250 bonds assuring that they would appear for trial during the April term of the Criminal Court.

Almost immediately after making their bonds, the raiders filed petitions asking a Federal Court Judge to hear their cases. The raiders contended that at the time of the alleged crimes they were officers in the service of the United States Government and were thus under Federal jurisdiction.

Not wishing to wait for a ruling from the Federal Court, District Circuit Court Judge N. W. McConnell ruled on April 16, 1878 that the case was a matter for the state courts to decide.

The ruling notwithstanding, the raiders had confidence that the Federal Judge would overrule McConnell.

Despite the indictments, handed down, the raids continued. On April 16, raiders destroyed two more illegal distilleries in Macon County.

In late April, United States District Judge Baxter ordered the transfer of the case to Federal jurisdiction no later than May 1. There was some speculation that the conflict between the courts might affect the frequency of the raids in the future. But this proved not to be the case.

The State Circuit Court did not immediately comply with the Federal Court. Instead, it asked the District Attorney General for an opinion. The DA opined that the Federal Court had no authority to take over the case because the indicted men faced charges of violating Tennessee law, not Federal statutes.

Based on the DA's opinion, the Circuit Court delayed complying with the order. However, the state court did not hold out for long. On May 6, the case moved officially to Federal jurisdiction. Circuit Court Judge McConnell disagreed with the move. He felt it the Federal Court was usurping the rights of the state court and he intended to fight it.

On January 2, 1879, Sheriff Price served Davis with three warrants issued by the Circuit Court in Macon County. Then Price took Davis into custody. Davis immediately filed a petition for a writ *of habeas corpus cum causa*, which Federal Judge Baxter granted. Baxter placed

Davis in the custody of US Marshall Wheat, with the understanding that Davis could go where he pleased under the bond he had already made. Davis could also continue to perform his duties as a Revenue Raider.

Judge McConnell continued the case until January 6, when attorneys for both sides would argue the constitutionally of the conflict between the courts.

Relations between the Tennessee courts and the Federal Court had grown so bad that Tennessee Governor James D. Porter felt the need to discuss it in his annual "State of the State" address in January 1879. He mentioned the Davis case in Macon County specifically. The Governor said he wanted the conflicts resolved in a "spirit of fairness and frankness."

Judge McConnell wanted the dispute settled with the Federal Court as quickly and with as little animosity as possible. In mid January 1879, McConnell wrote Tennessee Attorney General Benjamin L. Lea informing him that his court would not take further action against Deputy Davis until the United States Supreme Court ruled on the jurisdictional dispute. The Federal Court agreed to await the High Court's decision as well.

His legal troubles notwithstanding, Deputy James A. Davis (often referred to as "Captain") continued his raiding, On February 4, 1879, Deputy Davis and his raiders hit two more distilleries in Macon County. First, they destroyed the operation owned by Zach Thomas. There the raiders smashed a copper still with a capacity of 150 gallons and 15 tubs of beer. Davis placed the value of the distillery at $150.

Then the raiders hit the moonshine operation of John and Peyton Jackson. The raiders smashed 16 tubs containing 300 gallons of beer, and other items. The value of the enterprise was $75.

In November 1879, Davis led a series of raids in Kentucky. One of the moonshiners Davis captured was Tandy Fishburn. Fishburn had been ducking the revenuers since Davis arrested him almost exactly two years before. Like many wildcats in border counties, Fishburn moved back and forth across the state lines in order to dodge the long arm of the law.

In mid January 1880, Judge McConnell dismissed the indictments against Davis and the other raiders. The decision came in the wake of a compromise between the United States Department of Revenue and the Tennessee Courts. The closing of the case against Davis and the raiders allowed them an even stronger hand in pursuing moonshiners and bootleggers.

The raiding career of James M. Davis ended in Warren County, Tennessee shortly after that when a moonshiner killed him.

Sources

"Gainesboro." *Daily American*, January 17, 1880, page 1. Courtesy of the Tennessee Electronic Library.

"Capt. Davis' Last Raid." *Daily American*, November 12, 1879, page 4. Courtesy of the Tennessee Electronic Library.

"Capt. Davis' Whiskey Smashes." *Daily American*, February 8, 1878, page 4. Courtesy of the Tennessee Electronic Library.

"Conflict of Jurisdiction." *Daily American*, January 3, 1879, page 1. Courtesy of the Tennessee Electronic Library.

"Life at Stake." *The Daily American*, October 26, 1885, page 1. Courtesy of the Tennessee Electronic Library.

"Moonshine Matters." *Daily American*, January 15, 1879, page 4. Courtesy of the Tennessee Electronic Library.

"Revenue Raiders and the State Courts." *Daily American*, April 21, 1878, page 1. Courtesy of the Tennessee Electronic Library.

"The Conflict of Jurisdiction." *Daily American*, May 5, 1878, page 1. Courtesy of the Tennessee Electronic Library.

"The Governor's Message." *Daily American*, January 9, 1879, page 2. Courtesy of the Tennessee Electronic Library.

"The Revenue Raiders." *Daily American*, May 1, 1878 page 4. Courtesy of the Tennessee Electronic Library.

"Transferred to Federal Court." *Daily American*, May 7, 1878, page 4. Courtesy of the Tennessee Electronic Library.

"Two Macon County Illicit Distilleries Destroyed." *Daily American*, April 25, 1878, page 4. Courtesy of the Tennessee Electronic Library.

5. Seizure of Illicit Whiskey

At about 11:00 p.m. on December 11, 1878, Special Deputy Collector Chamberlain arrested James Cook in Macon County. Chamberlain seized a horse and wagon, and a "package" of whiskey from Cook. Chamberlain charged Cook with illegal removal and the possession of illicit whiskey.

On December 13, Macon County authorities surrendered Cook to Davidson County officers and they committed him to the Davidson County Jail to await his April 1879 trial in the United States Circuit Court.

Source.

"Seizure of Illicit Whiskey." *Daily American*, December 14, 1878, page 1. Courtesy of the Tennessee Electronic Library.

6. The Upper Country Raids

During March 1879, raiders swept through the northern counties of middle Tennessee. Many knew these counties collectively as the "upper country." Macon County was one of areas of the Upper Country where raiders struck. The locations of the raids described below illustrate how widespread moonshining was in Macon County in those days.

On March 6, 1879, Special Deputy J. M. Phillips and his men rode to Macon County's Long Fork Creek near the mouth of Dry Fork. There they found and destroyed Matt East's distillery. Among the items on the site were 8 tubs, 1,200 gallons of beer, 100 gallons of singlings, 2 bushels of corn, and a 150-gallon still. Phillips valued the East distillery at $300.

The second raid of March 6 took place on White Oak Creek about six miles northeast of Lafayette. Ed Green ran the moonshine manufacturing concern. Phillips and his raiders located 14 tubs, 1,500 gallons of beer, 2 bushels of cornmeal, 20 gallons of singlings, and a 75-gallon copper still which they laid to ruination. The value of Green's business was $200.

On March 10, the busy raiders struck about 10 miles northeast of Lafayette, at the distillery owned by James Walker and John O'Banion. The raiders captured 20 tubs, 2,000 gallons of beer, 100 gallons of singlings, and 5 gallons of malt. An informer had alerted the moonshiners and they removed the still before the raiders arrived and that reduced the value of the destruction to $75.

Another raid on March 10 took place on Little Puncheon Creek at the distillery G. M. Bandy owned. However, the clever moonshiner had gotten wind of the raid and had carried away everything except 8 empty tubs worth a measly $20.

Source.

"The Distillery Smashers." *Daily American*, March 12, 1879, page 4. Courtesy of the Tennessee Electronic Library.

7. Four Arrested in Raid

United States Deputy Marshall C. W. Strain got in the Macon County raiding act as well. On March 12, 1879, Strain moved into Macon County from Trousdale County in search of a still. He found it on the waters of Long Creek.

Strain captured a 150-gallon still, two mules and a two-horse wagon and harness. Strain destroyed thirteen tubs of mash, ten gallons of singlings, five bushes of corn, five bushels of malt, and three bushels of cornmeal. The haul's value was $175. Strain shipped the captured material to Collector W. M. Woodcock in Nashville.

Strain also arrested four men at the big distillery – Thomas Johnson, F. W. Napier, E. L. Napier, and Alfred Harper. Johnson owned the distillery and the other three were his hired hands.

Three of the men went before the United States Commissioner and he bound them over for trial at the April term of the Federal Court. The forth man went before the court on March 14.

Source.

"A Macon County Raid." *Daily American*, March 16, 1879, page 4. Courtesy of the Tennessee Electronic Library.

8. Barroom Blitz

While the Feds worked hard to curb the massive flow of illegal alcohol, there were still saloons operating legally in Macon County. Sometimes the saloonkeepers sought to increase their profits by purchasing the cheaper hooch offered by moonshiners.

In September 1879, Deputy Phillips raided the saloon owned by William Waldron. Phillips found and destroyed two barrels of wildcat whiskey.

The Deputy arrested the bartender and hauled him before the United States Commissioner. The Commissioner bound the bartender over to the October 1879 term of the US Circuit Court.

Source.

"Seizure of Whiskey in Macon County." *Daily American*, September 16, 1879, page 4. Courtesy of the Tennessee Electronic Library.

9. More Wildcats to Jail

The revenuers brought a steady stream of moonshiners into Macon County Jail. On October 4, 1879, United States Deputy Marshall J. M. Phillips brought in two more.

Macon County Sheriff, whether or not he wanted to, accepted B. B and R. W. Doss to his facility.

Source.

"Jail Notes." *Daily American*, October 5, 1879, page 4. Courtesy of the Tennessee Electronic Library.

10. A Puncheon Creek Still

After having dinner on the evening of October 1, 1879, Deputy Phillips rode out of Lafayette and into Allen County, Kentucky. There, on Puncheon Creek, he broke up two moonshine operations.

Phillips followed the creek back into Macon County and soon rode upon the distillery operated by Billy and Wash Doss. The Doss boys were busy making whiskey and Phillips surprised and arrested them.

The wildcat distillery contained 10 tubs, 600 gallons of beer, 150 gallons of singlings, 4 bushels of cornmeal, and a 100-gallon copper still. The operation was worth about $150.

Phillips said that the Doss boys acted tough at first, but they reconsidered later and promised that if they could avoid jail time, they would give up their illicit trade.

Source.

"Wildcat Concerns." *Daily American*, October 7, 1879, page 4. Courtesy of the Tennessee Electronic Library.

II. 1880-1889

The ten articles in this section cover the gamut of liquor related items. They range from the establishment of a legal distillery, to the politics of whiskey, to shootouts and killings, to the lives of two young men ruined by drinking.

These ten articles also indicate that despite the efforts of the raiders, moonshine operations in Macon County were growing in number rather than decreasing. However, despite being frustrated in their efforts, the raiders continued on their mission and arrested more and more wildcats.

11. Moonshiner Convicted

In early January 1880, the Circuit Court convened in Lafayette with Judge N. W. McConnell presiding. During the sessions of the court, several Macon County residents received convictions for a variety of crimes. A jury found one Macon County resident guilty of bootlegging.

John H. Morgan suffered conviction for selling liquor illegally. His fine was $50, but he did not pay it immediately. He exercised his right to appeal his conviction to the Tennessee State Supreme Court.

Source.

"Gainesboro." *Daily American*, January 17, 1880, page 1. Courtesy of the Tennessee Electronic Library.

12. Legal Distillery in County

Tennessee did not have statewide Prohibition. It was legal to operate a distillery in the Volunteer State, provided the operators met all applicable state and Federal regulations.

The Pitkin & Erwin Company decided to open the first legal distillery in Macon County and announced that production would begin on April 1, 1880.

Source.

"Lawful Distilling in Macon County." *Daily American*, March 19, 1880, page 4. Courtesy of the Tennessee Electronic Library.

13. Murder on the Square

A. The Murder of Hugh Sanders

The fact that alcohol destroys many, many lives is undeniable. The life and death of Joseph "Joe" Cartwright is a case in point.

While many happy events have taken place on the Lafayette Public Square, it has been the site of a number of tragedies as well. One such tragedy took place in 1880.

This story begins when the folk at the Church of Christ located on the Public Square in Lafayette (where Macon Bank & Trust is now) reported the theft of a demijohn containing wine they had stored for religious purposes. A demijohn is a large, narrow-necked bottle used to hold liquid. It is uncertain how much wine the bottle contained, but demijohns usually hold between 1 and 16 gallons.

Though only 24, Joseph Cartwright already had the reputation in the community of being an incorrigible drunkard and he came under suspicion for the theft immediately. When questioned about the crime, Cartwright denied any knowledge of it. However, the suspicion and a small bit of evidence, bolstered by some testimony led authorities to indict Cartwright for the theft in January 1879.

Joe Cartwright stood trial in April 1879 and a jury acquitted him. Though not convicted, the trial was hard on Joe and his family. His wife Martha Adeline Brawner Cartwright was pregnant with their second child (John Wesley Cartwright, born on July 29, 1879) and the fear of her husband going to prison took a lot out her.

Another young man, not too much different in age from Joe Cartwright named Hugh Sanders testified for the prosecution at

Cartwright's trial and this led to hard feelings between the two. Cartwright lived within the city limits of Lafayette and Sanders only lived a mile or two outside of town. The two had many opportunities to see one another. This only fueled their feud. Additionally, the bad blood between Cartwright and Sanders became common knowledge and the rumors and whispers it generated did not help matters.

The animosity between the two young men apparently caused Cartwright to leave Macon County for a short time between his trial for stealing the wine and the homicide of Hugh Sanders. Cartwright's family contended that Joe feared Sanders and that is why he abandoned the county for a few days. Others contested that statement and claimed that Joe left for other reasons.

Whatever the reason he left town, and whether or not Joe feared Sanders, the bad blood between the two men is indisputable. Sanders made threats against Cartwright in front of witnesses numerous times.

At least once, Hugh Sanders even threatened Cartwright to his face. Between the 3rd and 6th of October, 1880, Sanders came upon Cartwright at a fresh water spring where Macon County citizens often stopped to refresh themselves. Cartwright was drinking from the clear, cold liquid trickling from below the surface of the earth and did not notice his enemy riding toward him.

When Sanders saw Cartwright, he began to act in a provocative manner. Sanders abused Cartwright verbally and one witness said that he was certain that Sanders was about to draw his knife and stab Cartwright. For whatever reason, Sanders left his knife sheaved, but he did make an ominous threat. He promised Cartwright that he would see him again.

It was shortly after Sanders threatened him personally that Cartwright took leave of the county for a few days.

Apparently, Sanders feared that Cartwright would name him as the person that took the wine from the church. When he got wind of rumors that Cartwright intended to implicate him in the robbery, it enraged Sanders. He swore he would kill Cartwright if he made any such accusation.

After Cartwright returned to Macon County, Sanders continued to make threats against him. The last known threat Sanders made against Cartwright was on October 12, 1880, the day before the slaying.

The weather was nice in Lafayette, Tennessee on Wednesday, October 13, 1880. At least it was nice enough for young men to sit outside in front of the Johnson Inn on the town square and engage in conversation, idle and otherwise. Several young men including Cartwright and Sanders gathered in front of the hotel. The men were talking and laughing, but there wasn't any rowdiness, just "playful" banter.

Cartwright was drinking – probably heavily – and he had a gun in his possession. Contrary to the stereotype, Tennesseans of those days did not usually walk around with loaded pistols strapped to their hips. Many had pistols for home protection and most households had shotguns and rifles for hunting game, but it was rare to see anyone walking around town with a gun.

Neither Sanders, nor any of the men around him were armed, but Cartwright did not seem frightening to them. In fact, they decided to have a little fun with the intoxicated young man. One of the men said to Cartwright, "Does carrying a gun make you drunk? If it does, I'll get me one."

Then Sanders chimed in, "If it makes you drunk, then pass it around and we will all have a spree."

Cartwright didn't seem to mind the others having a little laugh at his expense. A few minutes later, the group broke up with Cartwright and Sanders going in opposite directions.

Between one and two hours later, Sanders and two other men returned to the front of the Johnson Inn. The owner of the hotel joined them. All four men sat and passed the time in idle chitchat. Sanders sat in a straight back chair leaned against the building. The conversation was jovial, but apparently not loud.

In a few minutes, Mr. Johnson saw Cartwright approaching them. Cartwright was still carrying his gun. Johnson turned to Sanders and asked him if he wasn't "uneasy" at the thought that Cartwright might attack him. Sanders replied, "No, we have been at odds, but we have agreed to drop it, and we speak when we pass."

Continuing to walk slowly, Joe came down the sidewalk towards where the young men were. When he was near, he stepped off the sidewalk and into the street to make his way around those between him and Sanders. Then he stepped back onto the sidewalk and stood directly in front of, and very close to his victim.

Evidently, Sanders didn't sense any danger, because he remained seated when Cartwright stepped in front of him. The lack of immediate reaction on the part of Sanders proved to be a fatal mistake.

Suddenly, in a loud, shaking voice slurred by alcohol an enraged Cartwright yelled at Sanders "Goddamn you! I suppose you have something against me!"

Then, before the unarmed Sanders could react, Cartwright raised, pointed his pistol, and pulled the trigger. The blast shook the windows of the buildings on that side of Lafayette's Public Square.

Cartwright was so near Sanders that despite his intoxication, he could not miss his target. The bullet ripped through Sanders' body, leaving him mortally wounded.

Cartwright had evidently not given any previous thought to getting away. First, he walked a short distance from the Public Square, but when he realized others were pursuing him, he started running across an open field in an attempt to escape. Despite his frantic attempt to exit the scene, subduing

Cartwright was easy. His captors wrestled him to the ground. They got him back on his feet, and hauled him to the jail. Once there, they turned him over to newly elected Macon County Sheriff W. T. Gray.

Hugh Sanders died within hours of the shooting and Cartwright stood charged with murder in the first degree.

Authorities transferred Cartwright from Lafayette to the Nashville penitentiary "for safe keeping" and back several times over the next several months. One of those transfers took place on January 11, 1881.

Cartwright stood trial in the Circuit Court. Judge N. W. McConnell of Hartsville presided over the trial.

Since there was no question as to the facts in the case, the only question was one of mitigating circumstances. The state of Tennessee, seeing no mitigation, maintained the charge of murder in the first degree and asked for the death penalty. Cartwright entered a plea of not guilty claiming his drunkenness made him unable to act rationally.

Joseph Cartwright came from a good family. His father, Enoch Cartwright (often referred to as E. G.) was a postmaster and served for more than two decades as Macon County Register of Deeds. Joe's family stood by him and his father, mother, Sarah W. Smithwick Cartwright and older sister Nancy, all testified in his defense. They all agreed that Cartwright had been drinking heavily for at least three years. However, considering his degree of addiction, it is likely that he had been drinking much longer than that.

Cartwright's family members also testified that Cartwright sometimes suffered from *delirium tremens* (*DTs*). *DTs* is the medical name for the withdrawals those addicted to alcohol sometimes experience when deprived of it. Of course, Cartwright could not have been suffering from *DTs* on the day of the killing, because he was drinking. However, it is likely that no one in the courtroom understood alcohol withdrawal.

Cartwright's family members also offered that Joe was "not of sound mind." Prosecution witnesses countered Cartwright's family by testifying that he was perfectly sane on the day of the slaying and that, in fact, he was always of sound mind.

Cartwright's father said Joe was "wild and very drunk" on the day of the homicide. According to Cartwright's father, Joe was out of his mind and worse than he had been for months.

The elder Cartwright had more to offer as well. He said he was attending his duties at the post office on that fateful Wednesday and soon after Hugh Sanders left the group in front of Johnson Inn, he came into the post office and asked for a letter. E. C. Cartwright said that Sanders behaved strangely while he was in the post office. The postmaster said Sanders kept his hands in his pockets the whole time, looked around nervously, and then walked quickly out of the building.

E. C. Cartwright continued that a few moments after Sanders departed, Joseph Cartwright entered the post office. The elder Cartwright told his son about his strange encounter with Sanders. He said he didn't like the way the man acted and he feared that Sanders was up to no good. Enoch Cartwright advised his son to go home before Sanders could work any mischief.

Joe promised his father that he would return home, but only after he talked to a merchant named Willie Claiborne. After he left the post office – and only a few minutes before he killed Sanders – Joe did walk past Claiborne's store and peered inside, apparently trying to locate the owner.

Sarah Cartwright said the accusations of his stealing from a church left her son depressed. She continued that, "charging him with stealing the wine, had put him below the respect of decent people." Perhaps Sarah Cartwright didn't realize that her son's continuous displays of public intoxication had caused "decent people" to lose respect for him long before the church had its wine pilfered.

All witnesses agreed that Cartwright was drinking on the day of the murder. However, testimony differed as to the extent of his drunkenness. Those testifying in his defense stated that he was very drunk, those testifying against him contended that he was "drinking, but was not drunk." Yet, even those testifying against him conceded that Cartwright was under the influence of alcohol to at least some degree.

After the lawyers rested their cases, trial Judge McConnell charged the jury on the subject of drunkenness as a mitigating circumstance:

"Voluntary drunkenness is no excuse for the commission of a crime, but it may be looked to, to ascertain whether the offense has been committed or not. We have seen to commit murder in the first degree the killing must be done willfully, deliberately, premeditatedly, and with malice aforethought. This requires certain states of the mind, and the question of the intoxication of the prisoner may be looked to, to see whether at the time of the killing he had these states of mind. Was he so intoxicated that he was incapable of giving the consent of his will to the killing, or of deliberating and premeditating the deed; if he was, then he cannot be guilty of murder in the first degree. But if he was capable of willing, deliberating and premeditating the deed, then he is capable of committing murder in the first degree, notwithstanding his intoxication, and it can be no excuse for him. The only effect that voluntary drunkenness can have in any event, is to reduce the crime from murder in the first to murder in the second degree. It is never grounds of entire justification, except it amounts to insanity, as will hereafter be explained to you."

McConnell continued: "If you believe, beyond a reasonable doubt, he (Cartwright) shot Sanders in malice, not intending to kill him but did do it, or if you find he was so intoxicated that he was not capable of that deliberation or premeditation necessary to make murder in the first degree, or you have a reasonable doubt how this is, you should find him guilty of murder in the second degree." That was the extent of the judge's charge.

On February 22, 1881, the jury, based on the evidence, the testimony, and the judge's charge, found Cartwright guilty of first-degree murder and the court sentenced him to death by hanging.

Cartwright's attorneys J. L. Roark and John G. Guild filed an immediate appeal with the Tennessee State Supreme Court claiming that Judge McConnell charged the jury in error. The Supreme Court heard the appeal in December 1881.

After hearing the arguments, the Supreme Court chose to render its decision based completely on previous court rulings regarding homicides committed by drunken men and not on the evidence of the Sanders killing. The justices ruled that Judge McConnell's charge was in error because he made the "whole effect" of Cartwright's "intoxication in reducing the killing to murder in the second degree depend upon whether the drunkenness was to such an extent as to render the prisoner incapable of deliberation and premeditation."

The High Court continued, that "a degree of intoxication short of this may, when taken in connection with the other facts, show that the killing resulted from a purpose formed in passion, and not deliberately and premeditatedly; and although there be no adequate provocation to reduce the offense to manslaughter, yet if in this mode the want of deliberation and premeditation appear, it may be reduced to murder in the second degree.

"In a case involving life, we do not feel ourselves at liberty to overlook this error, whatever we might think of the facts. The prisoner is entitled to a correct exposition of the law.

"The judgment must, therefore, be reversed and the cause remanded for a new trial."

Just because the Tennessee High Court overturned Cartwright's conviction didn't mean he went home a free man. On the contrary, Cartwright remained in custody.

The Macon County Sheriff drove Cartwright back and forth before between Lafayette and Nashville "for safe keeping" several times between the Supreme Court decision and the second murder trial.

When Cartwright did go back in front of a trial jury, the facts convicted him again. However, this jury did not give him the death penalty. Instead, he received a penalty of 15 years in the Tennessee state penitentiary at Nashville.

Cartwright's attorneys appealed the second conviction to the Tennessee Supreme Court as well. However, this time around, the High Court found nothing to overturn the decision and they let his conviction stand.

B. The Murder of Joe Cartwright

As is the case with most alcoholics, Joe Cartwright never went into recovery. After his release from prison, Cartwright continued to drink heavily for the rest of his life. Even on the evening of his death, Cartwright drank for several hours. Of course, when he bellied up to the bar on September 3, 1895, he had no idea his wife and four children would never see him alive again.

After drinking for a considerable time, Cartwright departed for his home on foot between 7:00 p.m. and 8:00 p.m. A little later, Cartwright's drinking companions heard two shots coming from the direction Cartwright was walking, but no one cared enough to investigate. The next morning, a citizen of Lafayette found the corpse of Cartwright in the road just outside of town.

The doctor that examined the body found that Cartwright suffered two gunshot wounds to the head. One lead ball entered his nose and exited the back of his head near the base of his skull. The second bullet entered the top of his head above his right ear and traveled downward. The murderer fired at least one of the rounds from point blank range because powder burns covered Cartwright's face.

Macon County Sheriff James W. King surmised that the shots the other drinkers heard were the ones that killed Cartwright, but he could not be certain of it. The Sheriff had no eyewitness, no physical evidence, and no other indication of who actually fired the fatal shots.

The investigation went nowhere and the Sheriff soon abandoned it. Thus, Joe Cartwright's murderer escaped justice.

Right or wrong, anti-alcohol proponents in Tennessee interpreted the Cartwright case as a telling example of why the legislature needed to do something about the alcohol problem. They contended that the Volunteer State needed to enact statewide Prohibition legislation.

Sources.

"A Cold Blooded Murder at Lafayette." *Daily American*, October 15, 1880, page 1. Courtesy of the Tennessee Electronic Library.

"An Alleged Murderer From Macon." *Daily American*, May 26, 1881, page 4. Courtesy of the Tennessee Electronic Library.

Blankenship, Harold G. *History of Macon County, Tennessee*. Tompkinsville, Kentucky: Monroe County Press, 1986, pages 29, 155.

"Brought Here from Lafayette," *Daily American*, January 9, 1882, page 4. Courtesy of the Tennessee Electronic Library.

"County Jail Notes." *Daily American*, February 5, 1884, page 5. Courtesy of the Tennessee Electronic Library.

Courier Journal, (Louisville, Kentucky), September 6, 1895.

"His Second Appeal." *Daily American,* February 6, 1884, page 4. Courtesy of the Tennessee Electronic Library.

"Jail Jottings." *Daily American*, January 12, 1881, page 1. Courtesy of the Tennessee Electronic Library.

Lea, Benjamin, Attorney General and reporter. "Cartwright v. The State" in *Reports of Cases Argued and Determined in the Supreme Court of Tennessee, for the Eastern Division, December Term, 1881, for the Middle Division, December Term, 1881, and for the Western Division, April Term 1882, Volume VIII*. Nashville: Travel Law Book Publisher, 1882, pages 376-386.

"Long Litigation." *Daily American*, January 9, 1882, page 4. Courtesy of the Tennessee Electronic Library.

"Mysterious Killing: Dead Body of Joe Cartwright Found in the Road near Lafayette." *The Nashville American*, September 6, 1895, page 4. Courtesy of the Tennessee Electronic Library.

"Placed in Jail for Safekeeping." *Daily American*, September 2, 1881, page 4. Courtesy of the Tennessee Electronic Library.

"Mysterious Killing." *The Nashville American*, September 6, 1895, page 1. Courtesy of the Tennessee Electronic Library.

"Sent to Pen." *Daily American*, March 6, 1884, page 4. Courtesy of the Tennessee Electronic Library.

"Taken to Macon County." *Daily American*, August 26, 1881, page 4. Courtesy of the Tennessee Electronic Library.

14. Revenue Men at Salt Lick

On January 29, 1881, Deputy Collector Elisha Chastain reported to Collector W. M. Woodcock that agents had destroyed six tubs of illegal beer near Salt Lick Creek in Macon County. The 720 gallons of beer the revenuers found had a value of about $30.

Silas Regan, who had fled Kentucky to avoid revenue officers, ran the illegal alcohol production operation. However, under Tennessee law, in order to convict a person of illicit whiskey production, the raiders needed to either get the moonshiner to confess, or catch him in the act. Regan never confessed.

Source.

"The Mission at St. Mary's." *The Daily American*, January 29, 1881, page 4. Courtesy of the Tennessee Electronic Library.

15. Wildcatters Shoot Deputy

The job of a revenue agent was a dangerous one. On March 18, 1881, US Deputy Marshalls Henry Seagraves and J. M. Phillips rode their horses from Lafayette in the direction of Red Boiling Springs. They had heard rumors of a large wildcat distillery in the area and they meandered through the deep woods in search of it.

After several hours of fruitless looking for the alleged still, the two men decided to break off the search and return to Lafayette. As they headed through the deep undergrowth toward the main road leading back to Lafayette, Phillips went down into one hollow and Seagraves went into another. Although separated by only about 200 yards, the men lost sight of each other.

Suddenly, two men, both on foot, confronted Phillips. In ominous tones, the men, both armed with rifles, ordered Phillips to turn around and go back. Before Phillips could react, one of the moonshiners fired his rifle. The lead ball struck Phillips in the arm. As Phillips began to dismount, the murderous moonshiner grabbed his partner's rifle and fired *it* at Phillips, this time, missing the revenuer. Deputy Phillips finished dismounting, drew his pistol, but he did not fire it. Instead, using it like a hammer, Phillips struck the moonshiner on the head with the pistol stock twice.

As the fight was in progress, Seagraves rode down into the hollow, and the moonshiners ran the 50 or 60 yards away to their distillery. The wildcats tried to hide behind their still house as the Deputies rode up. When the agents were about 40 yards from the still house, one of the moonshiners took a shot at Seagraves, but missed.

A person, unseen but evidently an ally of the moonshiners yelled out from inside the still house, "You had better get away from there or they will kill you!"

With that, the moonshiners ran from the back of the still house and took up positions behind a stack of logs about 60 yards away. Phillips fired once at the men as they hunkered behind the logs, but he did not hit anyone.

Feeling they did not have the weaponry to outgun the outlaws, and with Phillips being in need of medical attention, the raiders broke off the firefight and returned to Lafayette without accomplishing anything.

Phillips was a fortunate man. His wound was quite painful, but it was not life threatening. Upon returning to Lafayette, he visited Dr. Marlin Luther Kirby for treatment. Kirby tried to extract the bullet embedded in one of the bones the Deputy's arm, but he could not dig it out.

Source.

Blankenship, Harold G. *History of Macon County, Tennessee*. Tompkinsville, Kentucky: Monroe County Press, 1986, page 137.

"Raiding the Wild Cats." *The Daily American*, March 22, 1881. page 4. Courtesy of the Tennessee Electronic Library.

16. Raider Murdered

Less than three weeks after the shootout with the Wildcat moonshiners near Red Boiling, Deputy US Marshall Henry Seagraves lost his life in the line of duty. Seagraves was about 50, and he had a wife and three children. The federal government had employed him as a raider for about two years.

The first story of the murder came from a man named John Wallace. Wallace was a sawmill operator living at the edge of Macon County. He related that Seagraves intended to spend the night of April 8, 1881 at a house before returning home the next morning. Wallace said that five men called Seagraves out, forced him into the woods, and then shot him twice in the head.

The original story proved inaccurate, but the true story was almost as disturbing. On the morning of April the 7, Seagraves and a man named Cox went to Sumner County intent on making several arrests. They spent the entire day and much of the next in Sumner County, before heading toward home.

After nightfall on April 8, the two stopped about 12 miles west of Lafayette near the Siloam Church at the home of a man named Rutherford. Beyond resting a bit, the men had dinner while their horses fed.

After dining, in a hurry to get started home, Seagraves went outside to saddle the horses. Rutherford joined him. While the men worked with the horses, they heard pistol shots about 100 yards away near the cabin of an African-American man.

Curious, Seagraves asked, "What does that mean?"

Rutherford responded, "I don't know; the colored man has nothing to shoot with."

More curious than concerned, Seagraves told Rutherford, "Put out your lantern and I will go see what it is?"

Seagraves started in the direction of the cabin and when he was near, he called out asking if anything was wrong.

A voice from the cabin answered, "Who is there?"

As he continued forward, Deputy Seagraves answered with his name and possibly his title.

The officer never made it to the cabin. A shot rang out and Seagraves, hit in the chest by the bullet, died instantly.

After killing Seagraves, the murderers forced themselves into the cabin and ordered the owner to take a light and see what was outside. The intimidated man resisted for a few minutes, but eventually complied. He had not gone far when he came across the lifeless body of Deputy Seagraves. The frightened man returned to the cabin and told the criminals what he had seen.

The murderers ordered the man to go back outside and to drag the corpse inside the cabin. This time the man refused to help the murderers even upon threats of death. Frustrated, the criminals locked the man inside the cabin, took a lantern, and went outside themselves.

The murderers searched Seagraves, took his pistol, pocket watch, and whatever money he had on his person. They did not drag him to the cabin. Perhaps in an attempt to convince anyone listening that they were Native Americans, the murderers whooped and hollered like wild men as they took the dead man's possessions.

Later, when the authorities let the man out of his cabin he told them that four men came to his cabin before the killing and asked if Seagraves and Cox were at the Rutherford place. Then, the man went over to Rutherford's and looked at the horses.

The United States Marshall surmised that the motive for the Seagraves murder was robbery. The Marshall reasoned that the killers knew Seagraves probably had a lot of money he had collected in the performance of his duty as a revenue collector.

Strangely, the inscription on the tombstone of Henry Seagraves reads, "A revenue officer shot by John Bradley at a still."

Sources.

"Reported Outrage." *The Daily American*, April 10 1881, page 1. Courtesy of the Tennessee Electronic Library.

"Seagraves Murder." *The Daily American*, April 12, 1881. page 4. Courtesy of the Tennessee Electronic Library.

17. Phillips Wounded

United States Deputy Marshall J. M. Phillips was an impressive figure. He was about 40, a little above average height, very strong, muscular, and lean. He had light blue eyes, a lantern jaw, and a few sprigs of gray had sprouted in his beard.

Phillips was an old school swashbuckler, a fearless and determined Deputy, a man willing to spend days in hostile country and bad weather, to capture even the most desperate moonshiner. In short, he had the perfect personality for a Revenue Raider.

Phillips was also lucky – incredibly lucky. A wildcat moonshiner had once shot him in the chest with the bullet just missing his heart and exiting his back without contacting any major organ.

On March 18, 1882, Phillips barely escaped death again. Phillips was in the deep woods of Macon County searching for two specific moonshiners. It was about dusk as he rode slowly through the tall vegetation near a house occupied by the moonshiners.

Suddenly, the moonshiners stepped out into the open mere feet from Phillips. The Deputy stopped his horse and tried to draw his revolver as quickly as possible. He was not quick enough. One of the moonshiners raised his rifle and fired. The molten lead struck Phillips in the right wrist shattering the bone.

The second moonshiner raised his rifle, but Phillips spurred his horse and when it bolted forward, the moonshiner lost his aim. Phillips took the opportunity to return fire, but being aboard the startled horse and with his wrist shattered, it is little wonder that the Deputy's shot went wild.

Unable to reload their weapons without risking Phillips shooting them both dead, the moonshiners turned and spirited into the thick, quickly darkening woods. Phillips emptied his pistol into the shadows at the receding outlaws, but he hit neither of them.

Despite his wound, Phillips still had a job to do. He dismounted, reloaded, and continued his search for the distillery. Within 30 minutes, he had found and destroyed the still, but he never caught up with the moonshiners who had tried to murder him.

Source.

"Life at Stake." *The Daily American*, October 26, 1885, page 1. Courtesy of the Tennessee Electronic Library.

18. Liquor and Elections

Fourth Circuit Court Judge N. W. McConnell was up for reelection in 1886 and it appeared that he had a tough campaign ahead of him. In fact, it seemed probable that he would lose the election badly.

McConnell had spent his career on the bench in a crusade to suppress illicit liquor traffic in his circuit. He had, by all accounts, been somewhat successful at it.

A large group of people did not want moonshiners suppressed. These "liquor men" despised the judge and they wanted him off the bench. In fact, they were willing to do almost anything to supplant McConnell (including charging him with malfeasance) so that liquor could once again flow unencumbered out of the wooded hills of the upper country.

Source.

"Hartsville." *The Daily American*, December 7, 1885, page 7. Courtesy of the Tennessee Electronic Library.

19. Infamous Moonshiner Jailed

Macon County's James Patterson was one of Tennessee's most notorious moonshiners. In his time as a wildcatter, he accumulated 35 indictments (20 in Macon County, 13 in Trousdale County, and 2 in Smith County).

Federal Marshalls were almost desperate to capture Patterson, but he managed to give the slip for years. Patterson was so adept at avoiding capture that he grew complacent and it proved his undoing.

Patterson was a big catch by any reckoning and Federal Agents stayed on his trail. In early August 1888, United States Deputy Marshalls Joe Spurrier, Henderson Young, and F. H. Haynes went to the Patterson property at the head of Dixon Creek in Macon County and spent the night hidden in the moonshiner's tobacco patch. They waited patiently until about 10:00 a. m. the next morning when Patterson arrived with his gun and weeding hoe.

Patterson evidently saw no reason to take any precautions to prevent his being surprised. He put his gun down, and began hoeing his tobacco. When Patterson had moved a few feet away from his gun, the three Deputies rushed from their hiding places and endeavored to arrest him.

Patterson refused to surrender quietly. Instead, he attempted to make a run for it. Not willing to let such a big prize get away, one of the Deputies fired his pistol at the fleeing felon. The bullet clipped one of Patterson's ears and the blood and pain were enough to cause him to stop. The three Deputies took the fugitive in custody, and then hauled him before the Commissioner. The Commission bound Patterson over for trial and ordered him jailed.

Source.

"Many Moonshiners." *The Daily American,* August 7, 1888, page 7. Courtesy of the Tennessee Electronic Library.

"Over the State." *The Daily American*, August 6, 1888, page 7. Courtesy of the Tennessee Electronic Library.

20. Court Charges Forty-Seven

The "whiskey men" didn't care if citizens added to their incomes by churning out and selling moonshine whiskey illegally. Because of the apathy interdiction of outlaw whisky declined for several years. But 1889, saw an invigoration of Federal efforts to stamp out wildcatters in the Upper Country.

At the October 1889 session of Federal Court, 47 citizens of Macon County stood accused of various crimes associated with moonshine operations. This was an amazing number when one considers that Macon County did not have a large population in those days.

Some observers worried that the crackdown on wildcat liquor operations would damage the Macon County economy. The whiskey sold for $1.50 to $2 a gallon. Thus, the average still would generate the hefty sum of between $6.75 and $9 in income daily. This would mean that only 50 stills could produce in excess of $135,000 per annum.

Source.

"Moonshine Beams." *The Daily American,* October 27, 1889, page 7. Courtesy of the Tennessee Electronic Library.

III. 1890-1899

Raiding was becoming less and less newsworthy. Many newspapers simply stopped reporting anything except the most sensational stories about raids. The raids continued, however. The seven articles in this session prove that.

There are several instances of raids discussed in this section. One article also discusses the plans for a new legal distillery in Macon County.

21. More Arrests in Macon

United States Deputy Federal Marshall Tom Ballou spent about three weeks in January 1890 on the trail of violators of the revenue laws.

Deputy Ballou arrested several moonshiners in Macon County and transported them before the Commissioner who bound them over to face trial at the next session of the Federal Court.

Source.

"With the Moonshiners." *The Daily American*, February 5, 1890, page 3. Courtesy of the Tennessee Electronic Library.

22. Ballou Makes More Raids

Deputy J. B. Ballou made several more raids in Macon County during March 1890. He took some 20 bootleggers into custody.

While Ballou had not lost his passion for his job, it did discourage him that no matter how many wildcat stills he busted up, "that good ole mountain dew" continued to flow throughout Macon County in ever-increasing amounts.

Source.

"After Moonshiners." *The Daily American*, March 20, 1890, page 3. Courtesy of the Tennessee Electronic Library.

23. Three Convictions

Three citizens of Macon County received guilty verdicts in court on April 23, 1890. However, none of them received very harsh sentences.

Found guilty of illicit sales of liquor, Gilbert Wakefield received no penalty except court costs.

William Good received a conviction for illicit liquor sales. The judge ordered him to pay a $100 fine and sentenced him to 30 days in jail.

S. M. Kirby's conviction was for the violation of sections 3226 and 3279 of the liquor law. He received no sentence, but he did have to pay court costs.

Source.

"The Wildcatters." *The Daily American*, April 24, 1890, page 5. Courtesy of the Tennessee Electronic Library.

24. A Raid in RBS

On August 7, 1890, Deputy Joe Spurrier raided a distillery about three miles from Red Boiling Springs. There he captured and destroyed a still of 80-gallons in capacity, a cap and worm, six fermenting tubs, and a flake stand.

Albert Slate, the owner of the still, had dragged it into the woods and tried to hide it. Slate had not made any wildcat whiskey for some time because corn was scarce in Macon County due to a drought.

Spurrier made no arrests in the case.

Source.

"Wild Catters." *The Daily American*, August 7, 1890, page 3. Courtesy of the Tennessee Electronic Library.

25. A New Legal Distillery

Whiskey was such big business across the US that distilleries opened across the land.

Jim Loftis of Lafayette decided to get in on the hooch bonanza. He announced that he would open a legal distillery on May 7, 1894. He expected his business to produce 25 gallons of whiskey daily.

Source.

"Custom House Notes." *The Daily American*, April 21, 1894, page 5. Courtesy of the Tennessee Electronic Library.

26. Raid on the Border

On the morning of September 8, 1894, Deputy W. G. Rutledge and his raiding party rode out of Lafayette on a search for moonshiners. The remainder of the raiding party consisted of Deputies Tom Ballou of Nashville, W. H. Brooks of Dixon Springs, and two men Rutledge deputized for the raid, H. H. Newell, and J. F. Anglea, both of Lafayette. One or both of the Lafayette men guided the party through the Macon County woods.

The raiders traveled throughout eastern Macon County for the balance of the day. They even rode across the wild, rugged hill country of northern Macon County near the Tennessee-Kentucky line throughout the night.

About daybreak on September 9, the raiders came upon the house of Jim Reece. With military efficiency, Rutledge deployed his men around the house to prevent Reece's escape. Then, Rutledge burst inside and arrested the sleeping moonshiner.

The raiders then, again with the aid of their guide, went to Reece's distillery. What they found was one of the finest liquor producing enterprises in Tennessee, legal or illegal. It sported a brand new copper still capable of producing 50 gallons of whiskey a day. If running at full capacity, the still would churn out $30,000 in untaxed liquor annually. The country was too rugged to transport the still and Rutledge ordered it destroyed.

Rutledge learned that various moonshiners had produced wildcat whiskey on the site continually for at least the past five years. The moonshiners avoided arrest by moving the operation into Kentucky when agents from Tennessee got too close, then moved back into Tennessee when the heat died down.

Deputy Rutledge delivered Jim Reece to the Commissioner who bound him over for trial and then released him on bond.

Source.

"Mountains of Macon." *The Daily American*, September 12, 1894, page 4. Courtesy of the Tennessee Electronic Library.

27. In Federal Court

On October 22, 1895, The Federal Circuit Court in Nashville heard more than 50 liquor cases. Federal Judge C. D. Clark was as lenient as he could be with the moonshiners. He usually meted out the minimum punishment possible, or (sometimes) no punishment at all.

The only citizen of Macon County called before the judge for wildcatting on October 22 was Noah Fisher. Fisher was not in court. Judge Clark forfeited Fisher's bond and issued an arrest warrant for the moonshiner.

Federal Court continued on October 23, with Judge Clark forced to sentence so many moonshiners to prison that he filled the Davidson County Jail. In three days, he had sentenced more than 100 moonshiners to confinement, and neighboring jails had to provide adequate accommodations for 50 or so moonshiners.

Macon County residents before Judge Clark on October 23 included:

W. J. Jones, adjudged guilty and sentenced to 30 days in jail, and fined $100.

Elijah Gregory adjudged not guilty.

John Henry Law adjudged not guilty.

John Harris adjudged guilty, but the judge did not send him to jail or fine him.

Pierce Whitley adjudged not guilty.

On October 24, the Federal Court continued to churn along with several other Macon County citizens appearing before Judge Clark.

Davis Smith stood charged with selling whiskey at a picnic. He declared that he was innocent and put on a vigorous defense. During cross-examination, Smith's attorney accused a witness of drunkenness at the picnic. The enraged prosecution witness denied the charge vehemently. The witness claimed to have done very little drinking that afternoon. He admitted to consuming "only" three pints of whiskey at the picnic. The jury acquitted Smith.

F. P. Kirby failed to appear. Judge Clark forfeited Kirby's bond and issued an arrest warrant for the moonshiner.

Willie Jones found guilty, but Judge Clark him because he felt Jones had already suffered enough punishment.

Alfred Carver adjudged guilty, sentenced to 30 days in jail, and fined $100.

Morgan Wood adjudged not guilty.

One interesting thing that came out of the Federal Court proceedings was that moonshiners often used the United States mail to deliver illicit liquor to customers. Sometimes the mail carriers knew what they were doing and charged the moonshiners for their services. Other times, the mail carriers may have been innocent of what they were doing. There is no evidence that any mail carrier in Macon County ever acted deliberately as a courier for wildcat whiskey producers.

Another interesting fact coming out of the Federal Court was that illicit whiskey production was moving eastward. The number of those charged for making "Mountain Dew" in the counties of Clay and Jackson were considerably greater than in Macon County. Just a few years earlier, that was not the case.

Sources.

"Crowding in the Jails." *The Nashville American October 24, 1895*, page 2. Courtesy of the Tennessee Electronic Library.

"He Bought it to Drink." *The Nashville American*, October 25, 1895, page 4. Courtesy of the Tennessee Electronic Library.

"Queer Court Tales." *The Nashville American*, October 23, 1895, page 4. Courtesy of the Tennessee Electronic Library.

IV. 1900-1909

The changing of centuries didn't mean much of a change regarding the whiskey war. It continued unabated.

There were some notable differences than in the past, however. Tennessee Governors were more inclined than previously to pardon moonshiners. Additionally, Sheriffs were less likely to deal harshly with moonshiners.

One of the eight articles here would be humorous, if it had not ended with a man's death. In it, a frightened man mistook an extremely drunk moonshiner for a bear (See Article 34.).

28. Two More in Court

On April 17, 1900, two more Macon County residents stood trial in Federal Court on liquor charges.

Frank Brasel adjudged not guilty.

John Uhles adjudged guilty and fined $100.

Source.

"Lunatic in Court." *The Nashville American*, April 18, 1900, page 5. Courtesy of the Tennessee Electronic Library.

29. Macon Man Pardoned

I. N. Wakefield received six months in jail and a $50 fine for retailing liquor without a license. A good many people thought the sentence unjust and that Wakefield deserved a pardon.

The trial judge, the Attorney General, and several citizens of Macon county petitioned Governor Benton McMillin asking for a pardon for Wakefield. They contended that Wakefield did not violate the law purposely and that he was only "technically" guilty.

On September 10, 1901, the Governor granted the pardon and set Wakefield free.

Source.

"Two Pardons Granted." *The Nashville American*, September 10, 1901, page 5. Courtesy of the Tennessee Electronic Library.

30. Bootleggers Convicted

While liquor law violations were not the same big news as they were in the past, bootlegging had not disappeared in Macon County. On the contrary, bootlegging was on the rise.

In late March 1906, the District Attorney General was able to secure the conviction of four bootleggers. The most notorious offender proved to be an African-American man that had "worried law-abiding" citizens for several years. The court sentenced the man to six months in jail and fined him.

Source.

"Macon County Grand Jury Breaks Record." *The Nashville American*, March 27, 1906, page 5. Courtesy of the Tennessee Electronic Library.

31. Clemency for Macon Man

Wade Donoho of Macon County received a sentence of six months in the workhouse and a $50 fine for tippling (operating a bar without a license).

The trial judge, prominent officials, and Macon County citizens appealed to Tennessee Governor Malcolm Patterson to grant Donoho executive clemency. His defenders contended that Donoho suffered from "rheumatism, catarrh of the head, lung trouble and hemorrhoids" and that further incarceration would cause Donoho's death.

Patterson felt compassion for the convicted man and on December 19, 1907, the he granted the request and extended Donoho clemency.

Source.

"Clemency Exercised." *The Nashville American*, December 19, 1907, page 5. Courtesy of the Tennessee Electronic Library.

32. Sheriff Arrested

Macon County Sheriff James Ragland was a large and at 37, he was a youthful man. But he was no prohibitionist. In fact, he was a drinking man, and given to the mistakes that drinkers often make.

On the evening of January 21, 1908, Ragland was on Nashville's Fourth Avenue. He had been drinking heavily and there was some sort of altercation.

Nashville patrol officers Thomas and Hughes came upon Ragland and an argument soon ensued. Eventually, the police officers relieved Ragland of his pistol, hauled him to the Davidson County Jail, and charged him with drunk and disorderly conduct.

Source.

"Sheriff Locked Up." *The Nashville American*, January 21, 1908, page 2. Courtesy of the Tennessee Electronic Library.

33. Pardon of Bootlegger

William Carter was a poor man with a wife and four children. He had served two months of a three-month jail term. The court had also fined him $50 and ordered him to pay court costs.

The trial judge and several citizens of Macon County appealed strongly to Governor Malcolm

Patterson to grant a pardon to Carter. The Governor granted the pardon on September 14, 1908.

Source.

"Governor Patterson Gives Five Pardons." *The Nashville Tennessean*, September 15, 1908, page 3. Courtesy of the Tennessee Electronic Library.

34. Man Mistaken for Bear

Thomas Andrews had been involved in the bootlegging trade in both Macon County and across the line in Kentucky for several years. During it previous session, the local Grand Jury indicted Andrews for selling whiskey to a minor. In order to avoid arrest, Andrews skipped over the border into Kentucky.

Andrews continued plying his trade while in Bluegrass state. When Kentucky authorities began to bear down on him, Andrews slipped back across the line and surrendered to Macon County authorities. Then, while Andrews awaited trial on the first charge, another Grand Jury indicted him on two counts of selling liquor inside the County Courthouse. A jury convicted Andrews and Judge Joseph M. Gardenhire sentenced him to jail.

As already illustrated, Macon County Sheriff James Ragland was not offended by alcohol consumption. Andrews had a wife and five children and on the morning of December 25, 1908, the compassionate Sheriff agreed to allow the bootlegger to go home to celebrate Christmas with his family, provided he returned to the jail afterward.

Andrews did not go home. Instead, he spent the day drinking. About 7:00 p.m., Andrews staggered to the house of a widow named Coley and collapsed on her doorstep in a drunken stupor. It was a very cold evening and Andrews had cinched the collar of his long buffalo overcoat over his face.

Andrews made so much noise that it aroused the attention of the people inside. Widow Coley sent her young son to see what was causing the racket. The boy went to the door and called out. When there was no answer, the boy cracked the door open and looked out into the growing darkness to see what was outside. Startled, the boy slammed the door closed.

Going back to his mother, the boy said to her, "It's a bear, or something, with long wool all over it."

Now worried, the woman asked a visiting neighbor if he would go to the door and see what was outside of it. The man, a farmer named Thomas Deckmer (Decker?), picked up his shotgun and went to the door. Fearing that a vicious beast might attack him, he very cautiously opened the door a few inches and peered out.

The man could not make out for sure what he was looking at, so he poked the figure with his gun barrel and called out to it. The only answer he received was a snoring or growling sound. Deckmer poked the figure again and asked for a response. There was none.

The man poked what he now believed to be a bear for a third time and demanded it to go away. When there was no movement from the figure, Deckmer fired his shotgun at pointblank range, killing Andrews instantly.

On the afternoon of December 26, a Coroner's Jury held an Inquest and determined that the killing of Andrews was justified. There was some talk that a Grand Jury should at least review the facts in the case, but there was no paperwork filed in that regard.

Source.

"Very Unusual Sort of Killing." *The Nashville American*, December 27, 1908, page 2. Courtesy of the Tennessee Electronic Library.

35. *Is Prohibition Needed?*

The Prohibition movement in Tennessee was gaining strength. The proponents of outlawing liquor sales in the Volunteer State pointed to Macon County as an example of the "trail of blood" left by whiskey.

In Macon County, a drunken John Woodfalk had recently murdered Charles Nunley. Beyond that, in the last session of the Criminal Court of

Macon County, there were 105 public drunkenness trials.

On July 1, 1909, Tennessee adopted statewide Prohibition and remained "officially dry" until the repeal of national Prohibition in 1933.

Source.

Lewis, Frank W. "Political." *The Nashville Tennessean*, February 17, 1909, page 2. Courtesy of the Tennessee Electronic Library.

"To Test Validity of Prohibition Laws." *The Nashville Tennessean*, July 2, 1909, page 10. Courtesy of the Tennessee Electronic Library.

V. 1910-1919

Tennessee became "dry" officially in 1909 and that portended an increase in liquor raids. However, while the raids continued there isn't evidence that they increased very much in Macon County. Nor is there any evidence that a spike in wildcat whiskey production occurred in Macon County after the new liquor law went into effect.

What did increase was the political rhetoric involving the liquor laws. Politicians pitched the issue back and forth as if it were part of a game of horseshoes on a hot summer day. Several of the eight articles discussed in the section have political overtones.

Of course, raiding continued to be a serious business. One of the articles in this section deals with the possibility that a Deputy Sheriff used a minor liquor infraction to take revenge on an enemy.

36. Drunk Boys at County Fair

On August 20, 1910, the Macon County Fair came to a successful conclusion. The only downside was the large number of drunken teenagers that attended. Some of the people that observed the intoxicated lads stated their opinion that statewide Prohibition was the reason for the scandalous situation. The anti-Prohibitionists held that before, when it was legal to sell to adults, alcohol merchants would not sell to kids, but now that it was illegal to deal hooch to anyone, the bootleggers didn't care about the age of their customers.

The "Dry" segment disagreed with that Prohibition had anything to do with the problem. They pointed out that bootleggers had always sold whiskey to children and would continue to do so, regardless of the law.

Source.

"Fine Fair-Good Crowds." *The Nashville American*, August 23, 1910, page 10. Courtesy of the Tennessee Electronic Library.

37. Drunk Man Shot

Despite Tennessee's Prohibition law, those wishing to get whiskey could usually find it. On July 22, 1911, Marlin Maxey of Red Boiling Springs purchased a large amount of whiskey and got very drunk. Then, he spent much of that evening trying to start a fight with Max Jordan, also of Red Boiling Springs.

Jordan considered Maxey to be a friend of his and he tried avoid trouble with the drunken man. However, Maxey refused to allow Jordan to dissuade him.

Finally, Maxey attacked Jordan because of a cigar wrapper. Given no choice, Jordan shot his friend twice. One round struck Maxey in the forehead and the other hit him in the hip. Thankfully, neither wound proved fatal.

When Maxey sobered up, he admitted that the altercation was his fault, and he refused to press charges against Jordan.

Source.

"Shot at Red Boiling Spring." *The Nashville American*, July 25, 1911, page 4. Courtesy of the Tennessee Electronic Library.

38. *Democrats for Prohibition*

In 1914, the Tennessee Democratic Party expressed strong support for continued Prohibition in the Volunteer State and the strict enforcement of all the state's prohibition statutes.

On February 5, 1914, the Macon County Democratic Party left no doubt when it issued the following resolution,

> . . . *Be it further resolved, that we endorse the prohibition law and law enforcement measures on the statute books of Tennessee and we are opposed to the repeal or modification of them. We favor the strict enforcement of each of them. We also favor nation-wide prohibition.*

Sources.

"Macon Democrats for Law, Harmony." *Nashville Tennessean and The Nashville American*, January 8, 1914, page 2. Courtesy of the Tennessee Electronic Library.

"Ratification of Prohibition." *Nashville Tennessean and The Nashville American*, January 11, 1914, page A8. Courtesy of the Tennessee Electronic Library.

39. *Newspaper Bashes Liquor*

In August 1915, the *Macon County News* published an editorial condemning alcohol use. The editorial claimed that at the most recent two-week session of the criminal court, more than 90% of the cases "directly or indirectly" involved the use of alcohol.

Source.

"Liquor Did It." *Nashville Tennessean and The Nashville American*, August 3, 1915, page A4. Courtesy of the Tennessee Electronic Library.

40. *Rye Pardons Macon Man*

In 1916 a jury found Avery Harlan of Macon County guilty of tippling, sentenced him to 90 days in jail, and fined him $50.

The trial judge, District Attorney General, and several citizens of Macon County petitioned Governor Thomas Rye for a pardon for Harlan. Governor Rye granted a partial pardon, eliminating the jail term, but leaving the fine in place.

Source.

"Two Pardons Granted by Governor Rye." *Nashville Tennessean and The Nashville American*, May 24, 1917, page 12. Courtesy of the Tennessee Electronic Library.

41. A Victim of Circumstance

Police arrested Macon County's S. S. Jackson while he was moving some personal items. A search found a pistol and some whiskey among those items. Thus, Jackson was technically guilty of transporting alcohol and carrying a pistol, and he was so charged.

A criminal court jury, holding to the letter of the law, found Jackson guilty, sentenced him to 30 days in jail, and fined him $50 each for transporting liquor and for carrying a pistol.

The trial judge, the District Attorney General, and several Macon County citizens asked Governor Rye to pardon Jackson. They stated that Jackson was "a peaceful and law-abiding citizen, who had never been arrested for violating the law."

Governor Rye agreed and pardoned Jackson on February 14, 1918.

Source.

"Rye Pardons Victim of Circumstances." *Nashville Tennessean and The Nashville American*, February 15, 1918, page 1. Courtesy of the Tennessee Electronic Library.

42. Raids in Macon County

Johnnie Hanes was in his last year as Sheriff of Macon County and he went out with raids on distilleries in his county. His first raid was near Red Boiling Springs where they found and destroyed a still.

About two weeks later, Hanes and eight deputies raided a distillery about one and one-half miles from Willette in the Seventh District of Macon County. The moonshiners hid the still far back in the woods and deep in a hollow. The nearest house to the still was a mile away. Hanes discovered that Mrs. Luelle Goad owned the property on which the still sat, but there was no evidence that she had any knowledge of the moonshine operation.

The raiders found the distillery around midnight on July 19, 1918. The moonshiners were not present, but the raiders found 2,000 gallons of beer, some of it distilled and some of it ready to distill, several tubs, a furnace, and other items.

The Sheriff wanted to catch the whiskey makers badly and he waited on the scene until July 22 for them to return. Unable to wait any longer, the Sheriff ordered the distillery destroyed and he and his deputies returned to Lafayette.

Hanes related that there were many other wildcat whiskey distilleries remaining in Macon County. The Sheriff promised to flush out the moonshiners and to destroy their stills.

Sources.

Blankenship, Harold G. *History of Macon County, Tennessee*. Tompkinsville, Kentucky: Monroe County Press, 1986, page 155.

"Large Wildcat Still Is Captured." *Nashville Tennessean and The Nashville American*, July 21, 1918, page A5. Courtesy of the Tennessee Electronic Library.

43. Deputy Kills Prisoner

On the morning July 12, 1919, Deputy Sheriff Sam Hance served Homer Davis (age 20) with an arrest warrant for the rather minor offense of public drunkenness.

Soon after Hance arrested him, Davis broke away from the Deputy and tried to escape into the woods. As Davis ran, Hance drew his pistol quickly, and fired it at the receding man. The bullet struck Davis in the back, pierced his kidneys, and lodged near his spine. Davis died soon after.

The shooting outraged a good many citizens of Macon County and they demanded Hance's prosecution. The Grand Jury agreed and indicted Hance for the killing. The criminal court scheduled to open on July 21, 1919, had Hance's trial on the docket. However, the court allowed the postponement of the trial.

Hance finally went on trial in November 1919 charged with voluntarily manslaughter.

Hance's could not deny that he had shot Davis in the back, killing him. However, he said the killing was accidental. Hance claimed that he fired into the ground, but the bullet ricocheted and struck Davis who was by that time some 35 feet away from the Deputy. Contrary to Hance's testimony, witnesses to the shooting testified that the Deputy took careful aim before firing.

Another problem for Hance was that he and Davis had a contentious history with one another. For one thing, Hance had secured an indictment against Davis returnable to the November 1918 term of the criminal court.

Then, in 1919, Hance applied for and received an appointment as Deputy Sheriff of Macon County. As Hance prepared to move from Clay County to Macon County, someone burned his house by an act of arson. Hance felt that Davis had committed the crime. Hance swore out a warrant for Davis, but later dropped the matter.

Then, in July 1919, Hance secured an invalid warrant that was more than a year old and set out to arrest Davis. This led directly to the death of Davis.

At 3:00 p.m., on November 21, 1919, the jury returned with a guilty verdict and Hance received a sentence of from 2 to 10 years.

Hance requested a new trial, which the judge denied. Hance then appealed to the Tennessee State Supreme Court.

On February 5, 1921, the Tennessee Supreme Court heard Hance's appeal. The High Court found nothing to overturn the verdict and the High Court and rejected the appeal.

Source.

"Day's Rulings of State's High Court." *Nashville Tennessean*, February 6, 1921, page 6. Courtesy of the Tennessee Electronic Library.

Officer Fatally Shoots Prisoner in Macon County." *Nashville Tennessean and The Nashville American*, November 23, 1919, page 7. Courtesy of the Tennessee Electronic Library.

"S. H. Hance Given Prison Sentence." *Nashville Tennessean and The Nashville American*, July 13, 1919, page 5. Courtesy of the Tennessee Electronic Library.

"Two Weeks of Court Open in Macon County." *Nashville Tennessean and The Nashville*

American, July 21, 1919, page 5. Courtesy of the Tennessee Electronic Library.

VI. 1920-1929

With the advent of National Prohibition, Federal raiders felt energized – at least they did at first – and they pursued their prey with even greater intensity than before. The thirteen articles in this section illustrate that.

Local authorities continued to raid as well and Macon County almost lost a Sheriff to bullets from a liquor violator.

Tennessee Governors continued to pardon selected liquor law violators, sometimes upon the recommendation of judges, juries, and local sheriffs.

Macon County residents also had something to be proud of regarding Prohibition enforcement. The President named a local man to direct the Prohibition efforts in Tennessee.

44. Five Arrested

On January 17, 1920, National Prohibition took effect in the United States and more Federal Agents than ever spanned out across America interdicting the flow of alcohol. The effect of Federal Prohibition on Tennessee was not as a great as it was on some other states. The Volunteer State had been a dry state for more than a decade before National Prohibition took effect. Revenue Raiders had searched the hollows of Tennessee for years and they continued to do so.

On Christmas Eve 1920, Federal Prohibition Agents raiders captured two large stills in Macon County. During one raid, they arrested two brothers, J. P. and Bradford Hudson. The second raid resulted in the arrest of Charles Vinson.

Beyond raiding the distilleries, the Federal Agents stopped a buggy and discovered 30 gallons of whiskey. The agents arrested the buggy occupants, Lem White and Luke Morgan and charged them with transporting liquor.

The agents carried the five accused men before the US Commissioner at Cookeville. The Commissioner followed the usual procedure and bound them all over for trial in Federal Court.

Source.

"Federal Officers Make Raids in Macon County." *Nashville Tennessean*, December 25, 1920, page 7. Courtesy of the Tennessee Electronic Library.

45. New Prohibition Director

Word out of Washington on July 14, 1921 was that President Warren G. Harding would name

W. A. Smith of Lafayette to the post of Tennessee Prohibition Director.

Smith had practiced law in Lafayette for three decades, had been a Director of Citizen's Bank, had served in the state legislature, and had been a delegate to every Republican National Conventions from 1908-1920. He had been one of the strongest proponents of Prohibition in Macon County.

The pro-Prohibition elements in Tennessee were ecstatic at Smith's appointment. They felt confident that he would push for strict enforcement of the law regardless of any opposition he might receive. Smith did not disappoint them.

Sources.

Blankenship, Harold G. *History of Macon County, Tennessee*. Tompkinsville, Kentucky: Monroe County Press, 1986, page 142. Courtesy of the Tennessee Electronic Library.

Erwin, John D. "W. A. Smith Will Be Named Prohibition Director of State." *Nashville Tennessean*, July 14, 1921, page 1. Courtesy of the Tennessee Electronic Library.

46. A New Raider

D. E. Jenkins of the Red Boiling Springs and Pleasant Shade area was new on the job as a Federal Prohibition Agent. He made one of his first raids in September 1921. Jenkins arrested J. O. and E. J. Johnson near Gibbs Crossroads. Jenkins also captured 5 gallons of whiskey and confiscated an automobile.

Jenkins took the Johnsons before United States Commissioner Barnes for arraignment. The Commissioner bound the men over to Federal Court.

Source.

"New Raider Arrests Two And Seizes Car." *Nashville Tennessean*, September 27, 1921, page 5. Courtesy of the Tennessee Electronic Library.

47. *Two More Arrests*

Prohibition Agent D. E. Jenkins continued his raids with the aid of W. B. Stone. They had plenty of opportunities.

In early June 1922, the agents raided the home of J. L. Yokley at Red Boiling Springs. There they found ½ gallon of "white liquor" (that is, clear whiskey). Yokley denied that the liquor was his, but Jenkins and Stone arrested him anyway. United States Barnes placed Yokley under a $500 bond and bound him over to Federal Court.

The agents then went to Donnie Clark's store at Draper's Crossroads. The agents searched the store, but found nothing. During the raid, Jenkins and Stone saw Edgar Clark, Donnie

Clark's brother, running into the woods with something in his hand.

The agents chased Edgar Clark down and questioned him. The questioning led to the agents finding ½ gallon of whiskey hidden in a tree stump. Edgar Clark said the whiskey belonged to his brother.

Armed with the liquor and Edgar Clark's statement, Jenkins and Stone went back to Donnie Clark, who admitted it was his whiskey.

Donnie Clark went before United States Commission Barnes too. Barnes placed Clark under a $500 bond and bound the man over to Federal Court.

Source.

"Berries Or Not, Jars are Useful." *Nashville Tennessean*, June 7, 1922, page 9. Courtesy of the Tennessee Electronic Library.

48. A Christmas Pardon

Governors have historically granted Christmas pardons to a number of nonviolent offenders each year. On December 22, 1922, Governor Alfred Taylor granted 37 Christmas pardons. Several of the pardons went to Tennesseans that had violated the state's liquor laws.

One of those the Governor absolved of his sentence was Macon County resident W. B. Knight. Knight was serving a term of 60 days for Public Intoxication. He also owed a $50 fine.

Source.

'37 Freed From State Prison As Christmas Gift." *Nashville Tennessean*, December 23, 1922, page 1. Courtesy of the Tennessee Electronic Library.

49. Jenkins Continues Raids

Prohibition Agent D. E. Jenkins continued his raids, In March 1924, the energetic Jenkins, aided by Constables Tom Coulter and Sam White, raided a distillery 6 miles north of Lafayette.

The raiders captured an 18-gallon "outfit," 200 gallons of beer, and four "fermenters." The wildcatters were not present and the raiders made no arrests.

Source.

"Raiders Do Effective Work Against 'Shiners." *The Nashville Tennessean*, March 11, 1924, page 1. Courtesy of the Tennessee Electronic Library.

50. More Money for Raiders

In 1924, the Macon County Court (legislative body) decided to give prohibition agents a bump in the compensation. The Magistrates adopted a resolution awarding half of all fines collected from violations of the Prohibition law to the agent making the actual arrest.

Within hours of after the adoption of the resolution, Constable Tom Coulter, one of those agents deputized by D. E. Jenkins, arrested a man named Bray near Red Boiling Springs. Coulter found a one-gallon bottle of whiskey in Bray's possession. After a preliminary hearing, the authorities bound Bray over to the criminal court for trial.

In 1928, the Tennessee Supreme Court found the practice of county governments splitting fines in liquor cases equally with law enforcement personnel unconstitutional.

Sources.

"Dividing Liquor Fines With Sheriff Unconstitutional, High Court Finds." *The Nashville Tennessean*, February 5, 1928, page 8f. Courtesy of the Tennessee Electronic Library

"Macon County Offers Bonus in Liquor Cases." *The Nashville Tennessean*, April 12, 1924, page 16. Courtesy of the Tennessee Electronic Library.

51. Governor Pardons Sadler

Macon County resident, S. H. Sadler helped a friend. He drove his friend's car down a hill for him. In this case, the good deed didn't go unpunished. There was whiskey in the car and when a Prohibition Agent searched the car, he found it, and arrested Sadler. Mitigating circumstances notwithstanding, a jury found Sadler guilty, sentenced him to 60 days in jail, and fined him $100.

By June 14, 1926, Sadler had spent most of jail time, but paying the fine would have taken most of the proceeds from his corn crop that year. Sadler was a poor man with a wife and ten kids and paying the fine would have put a dire hardship on his family.

Macon County Sheriff Bill Blankenship, several Macon County citizens, and Sadler's wife petitioned Governor Austin Peay for a pardon. The Governor pardoned Sadler and ordered him released.

Sources.

Blankenship, Harold G. *History of Macon County, Tennessee*. Tompkinsville, Kentucky: Monroe County Press, 1986, page 155.

"Governor Pardons Macon Countain, S. H. Sadler." *The Nashville Tennessean*, June 15, 1926, page 3. Courtesy of the Tennessee Electronic Library.

52. Raider Shoots Self, Arrests 9

On May 25, 1927, Prohibition officers from Kentucky and Tennessee swept into Macon County and captured one of the largest distilleries ever found in there. The officers also found nine men on the scene and took them into custody.

Apparently, the distillery was a family affair as several of the moonshiners shared last names. The raiders arrested Joe, Ray, Odell, and Cordell Harlin, Jim and Barlow Hedgecough, and Callis Sadler, all of Gamaliel, Kentucky. They also napped Thomas Dobson and Elsie Craig of Red Boiling Springs, Tennessee.

During the raid, Travis Taylor of Glasgow, Kentucky arrested Thomas Dodson and started leading the moonshiner back to where the other officers were rounding up the other whiskey makers. Dobson broke loose from Taylor suddenly and tried to escape into the woods.

As Agent Taylor was drawing his pistol from its holster, the gun fired. The bullet tore through Taylor's left palm passing between the bones of his first and second finger. Taylor then fired at Dobson and the moonshiner, who was not hit, stopped, surrendered, and allowed the wounded agent to lead him back to the other revenuers.

Taylor's wound was likely very painful, it was not dreadfully serious.

Source.

"Raider Shoots Self In Mishap." *The Nashville Tennessean* May 27, 1927, page 12. Courtesy of the Tennessee Electronic Library.

53. Sheriff Gunned Down

In 1927, Virgil Frye was in his first term as Macon County Sheriff. He had already developed the reputation for being a fearless and vigilant peace officer, especially when it came to enforcing liquor laws.

On September 24, 1927, the Sheriff was on a raid alone near Willette, in eastern Macon County. Frye observed Earl Goad and a man named Fleming drinking whiskey in a corncrib near Fleming's home. Frye also saw one of the men toss a bottle partially filled with liquor away. Frye arrested Goad and Fleming, but what started as a minor affair soon turned into a life or death situation.

Following the arrest, the trusting Sheriff made a mistake. Goad had parked his car in the road near Fleming's house, and the Sheriff allowed the prisoner to walk over to the automobile. Goad reached into his vehicle, pulled a shotgun from the backseat, and pointed it at Sheriff Frye. Frye pulled his pistol but did not fire. Instead, he ordered Goad to drop the shotgun. Goad did not.

The two men then opened fire upon each other and after a few shots, Goad ran toward the Sheriff's car that was just a few feet behind his own. From the way Goad moved, the Sheriff thought he had hit the prisoner and he stopped shooting. Goad was not hit.

After taking up a position behind the Sheriff's car, Goad fired twice more. This time pellets tore into Sheriff Frye's chest, puncturing on of his lungs. Frye dropped to the ground and Goad skedaddled into the thick woods nearby.

Goad's drinking partner did not run away. Fleming remained on the scene and administered aid to the badly wounded Sheriff as best he could. The Sheriff was very strong; he never passed out.

Frye received transport and admission to Nashville's Baptist Hospital. While the wounds were not fatal in themselves, the doctors feared that infection or inflammation of his damaged lung might kill the Sheriff.

The shooting ignited perhaps the biggest manhunt in the History of Macon County, but it got underway late. Four of Frye's deputies were at a camp meeting revival at Cedar Bluff and they were not located immediately. After the manhunt did get started, scores of law enforcement agents and private citizens from Macon and the adjoining counties fanned out through the woods looking for Goad, but he avoided them.

Frye's wife Florence was at home very ill. She had recently had an operation and the authorities felt it wise that they not tell her about the shooting until later. Poor Florence Frye never recovered. She died on October 20, 1927.

Sheriff Virgil Frye did recover. After spending several days in Baptist Hospital, he returned home to finish recuperating. By November 1927, Frye was back on the job, and his number one target for arrest was Earl Goad.

During the evening of November 3, 1927, Sheriff Frye intercepted Earl Goad as the fugitive drove down the road. This time Frye was not alone. He had several deputies and special deputies with him. Those assisting Sheriff Frye were Henry Meadors, A. H. Andrews, Tilford Gregory, J. F. Hancock, B. C. Andrews, and J. W. Leath.

Goad did not offer any resistance and the raiders took the fugitive and a man with him, B. B. Donoho into custody. Donoho denied any knowledge of the shooting and the authorities released him. The judge jailed Goad and bound him over for trial. Goad later made bond.

Earl Goad did not go to trial until May 1929 when a jury convicted him and he received a sentence of one year in the penitentiary. Then, about seven months later a move began to free Goad.

Surprisingly, the leader of the effort to free Goad was the victim of the shooting, Macon County Sheriff, Virgil Frye. Frye stated that he believed that Goad was too intoxicated on the day of the shooting to understand what he was doing and that had he been sober, Goad would have never harmed anyone. Although the members of the trial jury had voted for Goad's conviction, they joined Sheriff Frye in requesting the Governor issue the pardon.

On November 12, 1929, Governor Henry Horton reviewed the pardon request and freed Goad.

Sources.

Blankenship, Harold G. *History of Macon County, Tennessee.* Tompkinsville, Kentucky: Monroe County Press, 1986, page 155.

"Donoho Is Cleared In Macon Hearing." *The Nashville Tennessean* November 7, 1927, page 12. Courtesy of the Tennessee Electronic Library.

"Horton Pardons Three." *The Nashville Tennessean* November 13, 1929, page 10. Courtesy of the Tennessee Electronic Library.

"Scores Search For Gunman As Sheriff is Shot." *The Nashville Tennessean* September 25, 1927, pages 1, 5. Courtesy of the Tennessee Electronic Library.

"Wounded Sheriff Recovers, Nabs Escaped Gunman." *The Nashville Tennessean* November 4, 1927, pages 14. Courtesy of the Tennessee Electronic Library.

54. Horton Pardons Gifford

The year 1928 was a leap year and Tennessee Governor Henry Horton used February 29 to pardon some state prisoners.

One of the men Horton pardoned was Macon County resident L. A. Gifford. Gifford had received a harsh sentence of six months in jail and a $50 fine from the criminal court for violating the liquor law. The Governor felt the penalty was too great for the crime and ordered Gifford released.

Source.

"Two Get Pardons." *The Nashville Tennessean* March 1, 1928, page 2. Courtesy of the Tennessee Electronic Library.

55. Hospitalized Man Charged

This incident did not take place in Macon County, but one of those involved had a Macon County address.

On April 30, 1928, in Allen County, Kentucky's Forest Springs Community, Orville Johnson and Hubert Vance had an argument "over some whiskey." Johnson lived in Allen County and Vance resided in Macon County, Tennessee. The argument escalated, and Vance shot Johnson. After the shooting, Vance hurried back across the state line into what he hoped was the safety of Tennessee.

Friends transported Johnson to the Graves Infirmary in Scottsville, Kentucky. Johnson was still there recuperating from his wounds on May 11 when Allen County Sheriff E. B. Mayhew served him with a bench warrant charging him with possession of whiskey. Johnson put up a $300 bond and continued his recovery.

Source.

"Hospital Inmate Is Charged for Bone Dry." *The Nashville Tennessean* May 14, 1928, page 3. Courtesy of the Tennessee Electronic Library.

56. Septuagenarian Pardoned

On November 17, 1928, Governor Henry Horton pardoned Macon County resident, 70-year-old war veteran Bill Holloway. Holloway was serving a sentence of 90 days for manufacturing whiskey. He also faced paying a hefty fine of $750.

The majority of county officials, including the Sheriff, Judge Albert Williams, and numerous local citizens had petitioned the Governor for the pardon. They pointed out that Holloway suffered from several infirmities associated with age. Besides that, they stated that his continued confinement would leave his large family dependent upon "public charity."

The Governor counted the time Holloway had already served against his fine. Then Governor Horton pardoned Holloway from the remainder of both his jail sentence and of his fine.

Source.

"Two Are Pardoned by Governor Horton." *The Nashville Tennessean* November 18, 1928, page 24. Courtesy of the Tennessee Electronic Library.

VII. 1930-1941

The 1930s were a time of depression, dust bowls, international tensions, and other major problems. Yet, the whiskey war continued in Macon County as it had in the past. Although Prohibition was unpopular in many places, it was still popular in Tennessee and nowhere in the Volunteer state was it more popular than in Macon County.

The raids continued throughout the 1930s, sometimes including gunplay. This section contains thirteen articles illustrating that the end of National Prohibition had little effect on the whiskey war in Macon County.

57. Danger at Easter Egg Hunt

The annual Easter Egg Hunt at Hartsville was a major event with people from around the mid State bringing their children for a day of fun. However, in 1931, the Easter Egg Hunt almost turned tragic.

The crowd at the event in Hartsville drew more than 1,500 people on April 4, 1931. There were smiles and laughter galore. Then suddenly, Ottis Gann, from Macon County, drove his car recklessly through the crowd. Gann sped on without checking to see if he had struck anyone.

Tennessee State Troopers Wayne Hargis and J. H. Duncan gave pursuit and followed Gann for several miles in a wild chase until they finally caught him. The Troopers charged Gann with reckless driving and then turned him over to the Trousdale County Sheriff. The Sheriff added charges of transporting and possessing intoxicating liquor, and driving while drunk against Gann.

The good news was that Gann did not hurt or kill anyone and the Easter Egg hunt continued despite the frightening disturbance.

Source.

"Three Arrested By State Patrolmen." *The Nashville Tennessean,* April 6, 1931, page 2. Courtesy of the Tennessee Electronic Library.

58. A Gigantic Still Captured

In the early morning hours of August 23, 1931, law enforcement agents, Deputy Sheriffs Ernest Ramsey and Will Smith, and Constables Hubert Tuck and James Sutton slipped across the line from Macon into Jackson County, Tennessee. There they raided a wildcatter operation on Hudson Creek.

The officers arrested Dewey Hudson, Gene Holliers, and Malcolm Massey, all of Macon County. The arresting officers also found "one of the most complete wildcat stills ever operated in this section." The still was a beauty.

It was copper and it had a capacity of 110 gallons. The officers confiscated 600 gallons of beer as well.

The Macon County officials turned the moonshiners over to Jackson County Deputy Sheriff, Harley Webb, who took them to the jail in Gainesboro. The men suspects then went before Squire W. S. Hance and Hance bound them over to the November term of the Jackson County criminal court.

Source.

"Three Caught in Raid." *The Nashville Tennessean,* August 26, 1931, page 8. Courtesy of the Tennessee Electronic Library.

59. Shooting over Stolen Smokes

People do stupid things when they are drunk. This was the case on Sunday afternoon, April 2, 1932. The stupid act almost turned tragic.

Wint Johnson was a married man with children. He lived in the Walnut Shade community. Johnson was drinking as he tooled around eastern Macon County in his car that Sunday afternoon.

Johnson stopped and gave a ride to William "Bill" Donoho and Doyle Hudson. He then drove them to the home of Bedford Newberry who lived near the Willette community. The three got out of Johnson's car, but an incident happened before they went inside.

Johnson, of course, was not thinking clearly, and he became angry. He accused Hudson of stealing his cigarettes and Hudson denied it. Suddenly, Johnson pulled his .25-caliber automatic pistol from his pocket, held it near Hudson's face, and snapped the gun several times. Luckily, the weapon, which was probably empty, would not fire.

Johnson, still intent on murder, ran into Newberry's house, grabbed a shotgun, and came back outside. Understanding their lives were in danger, Donoho and Hudson turned and ran, but before they were out of range, Johnson fired the shotgun.

Pellets struck Donoho in the back and Hudson in the heel. Luckily, neither of the victims suffered serious wounds.

Officer Hubert Knight came to the scene, arrested Johnson, took him to Lafayette, and deposited him in the Macon County Jail. Johnson faced charges of drunk driving, possessing liquor, carrying a weapon, and assault with intent to commit in the first degree.

Source.

Scott, Betty C. Meadows. *Macon County, Tennessee Obituaries and Articles Volume 1*. Lafayette, Tennessee: Ridge Runner Publications and Genealogy Research, 2003, page 54.

60. Prohibition Law Violators

On June 30, 1932, United States Deputy Marshall Morgan Stout arrested Fred Parkhurst, Arthur Wilkins, and Sam Nixon, all of Macon County and charged them with violating the National Prohibition Law.

Deputy Stout took the trio before the United States Commissioner in Cookeville. After a preliminary hearing, the Commissioner bound them over for trial in Federal Court.

Source.

"Trio Arrested." *The Nashville Tennessean*, July 1, 1932, page 13. Courtesy of the Tennessee Electronic Library.

61. Judge Tough on Bootleggers

Franklin Roosevelt won election as President of the United States on November 8, 1932 on a platform that included the promise to repeal National Prohibition. However, Federal Judge John J. Gore refused to ignore prohibition laws, popular of not.

On November 18, 1932, Gore handed down some tough sentences for violation of various Prohibition statutes. One of those Gore dinged was John C. Taylor of Macon County. Judge Gore awarded Taylor a term of 90 days in the Macon County Jail.

Source.

"Liquor Law Violators Find No Leniency Here." *The Nashville Tennessean*, November 19, 1932, page 12. Courtesy of the Tennessee Electronic Library.

62. Conviction Upheld

A jury in Macon County convicted Henry Hesson of possession of whiskey. As was his right, he appealed to the Tennessee Supreme Court.

On January 12, 1935, the Tennessee High Court rejected the appeal and ordered Hesson to finish his sentence.

Source.

Supreme Court Decisions Rendered." *The Nashville Tennessean*, January 12, 1935, page 6. Courtesy of the Tennessee Electronic Library.

63. Rumrunners Shoot Sheriff

The interdiction of illegal alcohol remained a big part of law enforcement in rural Tennessee in the 1930s. The flood of illegal hooch produced in, and passing through Macon County made it almost impossible for the

Sheriff and his deputies to intercept more than a small percentage of it. However, they never stopped trying.

About 1:00 a.m. on the morning of April 26, 1936, Sheriff Jack Creasey almost lost his life attempting to stop the transportation of whiskey.

The story began on Jennings Creek Hill near the Willette community when Constable Hubert Tuck and Charlie West began pursuit of a car transporting a load of whiskey. Unable to cut off the suspects, Tuck out got out of the car and went to call Sheriff Creasey who was at jail in Lafayette, and West continued to follow the suspects.

Constable Tuck telephoned Creasey and told the Sheriff that about the "carload" of liquor headed toward Lafayette on the Red Boiling Springs Road. Tuck described the vehicle as a Model A Ford Coupe. The Sheriff and night watchman Tom Moss waited for the bootleggers to arrive.

After several minutes of waiting, the rumrunners still hadn't gotten to Lafayette. The impatient Sheriff thought that their car might have broken down on the highway. Creasey and Moss then drove down the Red Boiling Road looking out for the bootleggers and their Ford.

About two miles out of Lafayette, Creasey and Moss saw the car coming toward them at a high rate of speed. Creasey attempted to block the highway with his car and Moss got out, but fell down while doing so.

The bootleggers pulled their vehicle around the stopped police car, and as they went past, one of the outlaws fired three shots at the Sheriff. Two bullets struck the Sheriff's car. The third bullet hit the Sheriff just above his left wrist, travelled up his forearm, and exited just below his elbow.

Sheriff Creasey and officer Moss returned fire, emptying their pistols at the fleeing vehicle, but not hitting the 'shine runners who were speeding toward Lafayette.

Shortly after the exchange of gunfire, Charlie West drove up to the Sheriff's car and then he continued the pursuit of the Ford. West caught up with his prey just as it entered Lafayette's Public Square. The Ford went to the right around the Square and West went to the left, cutting off the suspects at the entrance to Scottsville Road.

Perhaps luckily for West, the bootleggers had thrown their weapon out of their car immediately after firing it at the Sheriff. Unarmed they did not resist West, and he arrested them. Almost immediately, Sheriff Creasey and officer Moss arrived and Creasey cuffed the suspects. Inside the Ford, the Sheriff found kegs containing 35 gallons of liquor.

After placing the bootleggers in jail, Creasey consented to allowing Dr. D. D. Howser treat him. Howser determined that the wound was not life threatening. The Sheriff made a complete recovery.

Upon questioning, the arrested men identified themselves as Raymond Rich and

Jim Renfroe, of Scottsville, Kentucky. Rich said he had a wife and two children. Renfroe had several motherless children. The pair said they had borrowed the car in order to go to Gallatin for Renfroe's wedding.

Later on April 26, Rich and Renfroe went before Squire S. F. Jones. The men admitted to having the liquor, but they denied shooting the Sheriff. Jones set bond for the two accused at $1,000 for each count. They could not make the bail and Sheriff Creasey lodged them in the county jail until the July term of the criminal court.

A jury convicted Rich and Renfroe on charges of possessing and transporting liquor and assault with a deadly weapon, with intent to commit first-degree murder. But the men served short prisons terms considering the gravity of their crimes. They received sentences of three to five years each.

As this chapter and other chapters illustrates, the danger involved in the Sheriff's job. Ironically, at the time the criminals shot Creasey, the Sheriff of Macon County received very little for his services. He did collect commissions and fees, and he did get free room and board in an apartment provided for him and his family at the jail. But that was about it.

That changed to a small degree in January 1937. State Senator Merlin A. West, who was from Macon County, proposed legislation to help the Macon County Sheriff. West's bill proposed to pay Macon County Sheriffs $60 per month plus the commissions they already received.

The legislature passed the bill on January 21, 1937 and the Governor Gordon Browning signed it a week later.

The $720 yearly spike in pay made the Sheriff's job a little more attractive, if not exactly lucrative. Even after the raise, the Sheriff remained one of the lowest paid governmental officials in Macon County.

Sources.

Private Acts of the State of Tennessee Passed by the Seventieth General Assembly Regular Session, 1937 Volume I. Nashville: Printing Department of the Tennessee Industrial School, 1937, pages 265-266.

Scott, Betty C. Meadows. *Macon County, Tennessee Obituaries and Articles Volume 1.* Lafayette, Tennessee: Ridge Runner Publications and Genealogy Research, 2003, page 161.

"Seven Clemency Pleas Receive Approval Of Parole Board." *The Nashville Tennessean*, January 5, 1938, page 9. Courtesy of the Tennessee Electronic Library.

"Two Men Held." *The Nashville Tennessean*, May 1, 1936, page 32. Courtesy of the Tennessee Electronic Library.

64. Three Big Liquor Raids

Less than a month after bootleggers wounded him, Sheriff Creasey was back at work leading raids on illicit liquor operations.

On May 21, 1936, officers from Macon County raided three stills and confiscated 1,100 gallons of beer and 12 gallons of newly manufactured moonshine whiskey. The officers also captured 2 copper stills and arrested 4 moonshiners.

The first raid by agents of Macon County took place in Macon's Fourth District and netted 300 gallons of beer and 2$^{1/2}$ gallons of whiskey. The operators of the facility escaped arrest.

The second raid was in the Macon County's Fifth District. The raiders arrested R. L. Price and his son, Buddie and confiscated 500 gallons of beer, 5$^{1/2}$ gallons of new whiskey, and found a shiny new 50-gallon copper still. Squire Carl White set bond for Price and his son at $500 each.

The third raid also took place in the Fifth District. Macon County officers found 300 gallons of beer, 4 gallons of moonshine, and a 50-gallon still. The county officers arrested Nathan Blankenship and his son Galen during the raid. Squire S. F. Jones set bond for the two men at $250 each.

Those law enforcement agents taking part in the three raids were Sheriff Creasey and deputies O. E. Bentle, Ed Sanders, Henry Williamson, and G. I. Wooten.

Source Consulted.

"4 Arrested in Liquor Raids." *The Nashville Tennessean*, May 22, 1936, page 9. Courtesy of the Tennessee Electronic Library.

65. Ellis Pardoned

The criminal court of Macon County found Charlie Ellis guilty of possessing liquor and fined him $100, $75 of which it put on "suspended payment."

On August 21, 1936, Governor Hill McAlister pardoned Ellis from paying the fine.

Source.

"Two Are Pardoned." *The Nashville Tennessean*, August 22, 1936, page 9. Courtesy of the Tennessee Electronic Library.

66. A Big Whiskey Shipment

The number of large liquor shipments captured had declined, but in March 1937, Sheriff Jack Creasey captured one.

About 2:00 a.m., on March 13, 1937, Sheriff Creasey and Sumner County Deputy Ollie Gregory stopped a truck with two occupants on top Long Hungry Hill. The two men inside the truck were Richard Abernathy and Thomas Robinson. Both men resided in Louisville, Kentucky.

Upon searching the truck, the officers found 70 gallons of bootleg whiskey. They destroyed 65 gallons of the whiskey and saved 5 gallons for evidence. They then arrested Abernathy and Robinson, took them to Lafayette, and locked them in the county jail.

Source.

Scott, Betty C. Meadows. *Macon County, Tennessee Obituaries and Articles Volume 2.* Lafayette, Tennessee: Ridge Runner Publications and Genealogy Research, 2003, page 15.

67. Macon County Votes Dry

The United States repealed National Prohibition in December 1933. However, the repeal did overturn Tennessee's state liquor laws and the majority of them were still in place in 1937.

Tennessee Governor Gordon Browning favored abolishing Tennessee's liquor laws entirely. To that end, he convinced the legislature to schedule a statewide referendum on the question of the repeal liquor laws in the Volunteer State. Browning promised that after the pro-liquor forces prevailed, he would call a special session of the Tennessee Legislature to remove the liquor laws from the books.

The vote took place on September 23, 1937 and to the Governor's surprise and chagrin, the anti-liquor forced prevailed in a big way. Dry forces won the referendum by a count of two to one.

After the voters had spoken, the anti-liquor forces demanded that Browning respect the result. They held that Browning should now enforce the liquor laws with the same energy and passion that he had intended to employ in repealing them had the liquor men won. The Governor did not commit to doing so.

In Macon County, the citizens that went to the polls voted overwhelmingly for the liquor laws. The astounding vote in the county was 1,098 for keeping the laws in place and only 68 for their repeal. The astounding 94 percent in favor of retention of the liquor laws left no doubt of the views of Macon County voters.

Sources.

"Drys Win Easily In Light Vote." *The Nashville Tennessean*, September 24, 1937, page 9. Courtesy of the Tennessee Electronic Library.

Scott, Betty C. Meadows. *Macon County, Tennessee Obituaries and Articles Volume 2*. Lafayette, Tennessee: Ridge Runner Publications and Genealogy Research, 2003, pages 44-45.

68. *Governor Pardons Caruthers*

Mont Caruthers went to jail in March 1938 on several charges. He faced paying fines on each of the charges as well.

After receiving a petition, Governor Gordon Browning pardoned Caruthers and relieved of every charge except for a fine for drunk driving.

Source.

"Four Pardoned Two Get Commutations." *The Nashville Tennessean*, July 28, 1938, page 7. Courtesy of the Tennessee Electronic Library.

69. *Raiders Kill Suspect*

While America's entrance into war World II loomed, the Whiskey War continued and the raiders continued the zealous pursuit of their jobs. Sometimes raiders were tragically overzealous.

Silas Anderson was an officer of the Federal Alcohol Tax Unit working out of Cookeville, Tennessee. Anderson had deputized Macon County Constable E. T. Keen giving the Constable the highfaluting title of "federal posseman." On January 18, 1941, Anderson and Keen were in Red Boiling Springs attempting to arrest Ralph Clay Witcher (age 28).

A "scuffle" ensued between Anderson and the suspect. A pistol discharged and Witcher fell mortally wounded. Constable Keen stated that the weapon fired accidently and that there was no intent to shoot Witcher. A Macon County Grand Jury did not believe the story and indicted both Anderson and Keen on murder charges.

Anderson and Keen, thinking they had a better chance of acquittal before a federal panel, petitioned to have the case moved to Federal Court. After considering the matter, on March 19, 1941, Federal Judge Elmer D. Davis ordered the case transferred to his jurisdiction.

On April 10, the Federal Court in Cookeville scheduled the trial of Anderson and Keen for June 10, 1941. But when the case came before it, the Federal Court refused to return a murder conviction against the two men. Silas Anderson remained on the job deep into the 1950s.

For their part, the Witcher family, and many others in Macon County, felt the Federal Court decision was unjust.

Sources.

"Cookeville Court Docket Prepared." *The Nashville Tennessean*, April 11, 1941, page 28. Courtesy of the Tennessee Electronic Library.

"Paul and Silas Theory." *The Nashville Tennessean*, February 26, 1954, page 28. Courtesy of the Tennessee Electronic Library.

"U.S. Court to hear Slaying Case." *The Nashville Tennessean*, March 21, 1941, page

26. Courtesy of the Tennessee Electronic Library.

Conclusion

The whiskey war did not end in 1941. On the contrary, bootleggers and moonshiners stayed around for decades and perhaps they continue to operate in Macon County to this day.

There is no doubt that public drunkenness, drunk driving, and other problems associated with alcohol use and misuse still abound and that the struggle to deal with the social ills associated with alcohol remains a point of unfinished business.

Photos

Moonshine Still from 1936 (Public Domain)

Joe Cartwright   *Still from 1878 (Public Domain)*

About the Author

CL Gammon has had a life-long fascination with the written word. This fascination has led to his becoming an award-winning author of more than sixty books. Gammon, who studied Political Science at Tennessee Technological University and History and Government at Hillsdale College, has entertained and educated readers for two decades. Several universities, including the State University of New York and the University of Akron, have used his books as course material. In addition, articles written by Gammon have appeared in more than a dozen publications. Gammon has also written for his hometown newspaper, The Macon County Times. Gammon lives in Lafayette, Tennessee.

Index